CW00848125

The Way You N

Says It All

JESSICA BLACKBOND

ISBN-13: 978-1717414984

ISBN-10: 1717414982

DEDICATION

For all the people who stand tall

with kindness and warmth.

You know who you are

because you shine.

CONTENTS

ACKNOWLEDGMENTS

Thank you to all the people who have supported my idea of 'The Way You Move Says It All'. In no particular order, except for my mum Cassie, who is first because her consistent enthusiasm and passion for this book has been wonderfully wonderful! Lady Rachel for encouraging me and always vocally believing and trusting that this will happen! My brother cousin Craig for his 'Pillow Pilates' inspiration; Ivo for listening, helping and editing without asking for anything in return; Lewis and Matt for understanding my mind; Maxine for feeding me, proof reading, and editing; Denise, Valerie, James and Mr Liu for their stories that I share; All my family and friends back home who are in my heart; Holly Tse at www.chinesefootreflexology.com for her kindness and inspiration of Dragon Spirit; And all the people I have spoken with and learnt from throughout my 16+ year career.

Introduction

Everything Is Connected To Everything

Congratulations on starting your journey towards sparkling, passionate, stimulating, dynamic and dazzling health!

This book is about your posture, fundamentally. It is a collaboration of information I have gathered together from my 16+ years 'Movement Therapist' work. To tell you the details of what I have come to realise about posture, it is best to tell you stories of some of those whose lives have been affected by poor posture and the results they have gained from correcting it. So each chapter contains a short story based on real life people whom I have had the pleasure of helping.

Each chapter also gives an overview of your body: body anatomy and physiology, and the body systems that are connected to specific areas associated with the stresses of daily life. Here I tell you the Traditional Chinese Medicine theory of how these body structures are connected to natures elements and how all five elements work together to keep you balanced and fit. With mindful self-help exercises and Pilates movement routines to perform in bed before you start your day, you are gaining an easily doable holistic approach to improving your vibrant health.

In these sections I give you short journal writing tasks, so you will need a notebook and pen close by. I recommend you copy the 'Wu Xing Interactions' diagram, found in 'The Wu Xing' chapter, into your notebook for easy reference as you read.

The chapters are broken down into four categories:

Engage, Experience, Energise, and Execute. To make your learning clear and easy to 'digest', I have designed the categories to be mini books contained within a bigger book, contained within one large book. A bit like putting a Russian Doll together again. You've got the little doll, which goes inside the bigger doll, which sits inside the even bigger doll. So here you've got a story within a story, which when put together makes one beautiful story.

The final two chapters contain easy to follow reference diagrams and the full Pillow Pilates Morning Movement Routine instructions, so you can enjoy the book without worrying about having to learn the information within each chapter.

This opening chapter tells of an ancient Chinese Tao folktale and introduces you to some of the concepts you will learn more about as we progress through your journey of discovering why your posture is affecting your natural sparkle, and how easy it is to effectively hold yourself differently to feel alive and kicking again.

The ancient story began thousands of years ago in China when men, women and children lived in tribes under the protection and guidance of animal spirits.

In ancient times, man's fear of natural disasters and a sense of dependence upon the natural world made man pray for some supernatural power which could control and keep humanity safe from harm.

People who lived in woodlands embraced the spirit of the fish; whose endurance could protect them from the forest watershed during spring rainfall.

Those who lived on agricultural land adopted the bird, who protected man from the summer heat fires with the breath of wind beneath their wings.

Men who travelled the earth were protected by the serpent which silently glided from one place to another with beautiful alignment.

Those who began working with metal chose the horse, whose strength of mind and body co-ordination helped man through the autumn fall.

And humans who lived near water swore by the shell-like strength and control of the ox, who could plunge through mud and swim through rivers even during the cold months of winter.

The people lived powerfully; each satisfied in happiness, protected against ill health and strong in mind and body under the guidance from their animal spirit.

Until one day a huge "BOOM" shook the land and divided the earth into two – heaven (yang) rose and the underworld, named earth (yin), dropped.

The only way the people could survive was to unite. And unite they did, along with their animal spirit to protect them.

Now that the tribes had become one, they decided to create a creature that would protect and guide all the people.

So they took the head of the ox, the spine of the serpent, the legs of the horse, the wings of the bird and the scales of the fish and they called this fabulous creature... The Dragon.

The people lived together for many centuries and built great empires, empowered by the connection they had to the dragon. The dragon became a symbol of heaven and decorated palaces, furniture and clothing across the globe. And still across the world today the dragon is regarded as a symbol of power, strength and luck; for people who are worthy of it.

Now, you might say "Great story, Jessica. But what has it got to do with posture?" And I would say "Everything!"

Take a look around yourself. People watch. Really look and notice people's movements. What do you see? People looking strong and agile, free of common illness and tiredness? I'm guessing not. And I bet, if you were to ask each of those people, they would tell you that they have at some point dreamed of looking fitter and feeling better, but they don't have the time, just yet, to exercise regularly.

I've heard people say it to me so often! And I've said in response "Rubbish! How many hours do you spend in bed each night? Can you spare 10 minutes before sleep, or 10 minutes before getting out of bed? Sure you can… So allow yourself that time to do a few simple Pillow Pilates exercises."

You see, we could all have the endurance of the fish, breath of the bird, alignment of the serpent, co-ordination of the horse and control of the ox, just as man did in ancient times. We just need to learn how to connect to it again...

Endurance Of The Fish

Embrace Your Yin and Yang for Life Force Qi

Connecting your liver and gallbladder

with your lumbar muscles and nervous system

to the element wood for continual

smooth flowing qi.

"Movement never lies."

- Martha Graham

I met Denise by complete chance at Shanghai Pudong Airport. As is typical with internal flights the departure time had been delayed by several hours, so I had treated myself to a coffee and a blueberry muffin, that looked nothing like blueberry or cake. But that's another story.

Anyway, Denise was travelling home to Chengdu, looking forward to her new life in retirement and spending quality time with her husband and grown up children since she had just said farewell to her previous life as a Monday to Friday International Event Manager in Suzhou. I was heading back to Chengdu after attending a Traditional Chinese Medicine (TCM) Wu Xing conference (you'll learn about the Wu Xing shortly). It was funny how we got talking because we were both exhausted and in no state to consider holding a four hour conversation, and similarly we had no idea that we would consequently meet each Wednesday for six weeks to work on easing Denise's lower back pains.

Our conversation started like this:

Denise: "I'm heading to the bin, would you like me to take your rubbish?"

Me: "Oh, thank you. Er… Yes please."

Denise: "It'll do me good to move. My back is killing me."

Me: "Oh dear."

For the record, I did say this with compassion. I just don't usually follow up asking people questions about their health for fear of appearing as a 'smart arse'.

Denise: "57 years old and already a geriatric! Car accident. 10 years ago though. Half my spleen was removed and now I suffer with terrible lower back pain. I'm so tired, my eye keeps bloody twitching."

As she spoke she rubbed her right eye with her index finger. I'm not kidding. I smiled when I realised what I was watching.

You see, interestingly in TCM, ligament or tendon pain (Denise's lower back pain), eye twitching and tiredness are common symptoms of a yin deficiency in the liver, which is often retained with poor posture.

Denise had a nice figure. She clearly looked after herself and took pride in her appearance. I could see her problem though. And to be honest, it looked like a pretty big problem.

Two hours into conversation, I'm crouched down to Denise's pelvis area, my right hand on her lower back, my right elbow gently pressing her tailbone, my left hand on her lower abdominals and my left forearm aligning her hips.

Me: "Breathe in" hmmmmmm "Take a long breath out. Exhale." ahhhhhh. "That's it, yes. There you go… You've got it!"

Denise: "Ah ha! Yes I totally feel that! Wow!"

Denise had lumbar lordosis. The natural internal curve of her lower spine was way too exaggerated which meant that she was sticking her bum out, like a duck. Duck bum.

Over time, the muscles surrounding her lumbar region (lower back area) had shortened and contracted, and her psoas muscle had become over stretched, which you'll learn about soon.

Denise needed to learn how to tilt her pelvis in-line again. It's a simple change, and when I assisted her in the airport waiting lounge, I loved seeing the expression on her face. A look of complete understanding. A 'lightbulb moment' I like to call it.

Denise told me she had suffered terrible lower back pains for years, but had noticed it a lot more in recent years, possibly due to hormonal changes, her body getting older and her non-stop busy lifestyle. She told me she had surrendered to the pains a few years back and managed it by taking mild pain relief medication. Although she'd love to travel more for leisure, she felt that the regular return weekend flights from Suzhou to Chengdu had made her back worse, and so now she'd prefer to not travel.

What a pity, I thought.

Engage Your Beam

Principle of Lower Region Powerful Posture

"Movement never lies" I heard that on my first day in dance training. Martha Graham was, in the mid 1900's up to present day, the female pioneer of western contemporary dance. Also known as 'The Mother of Modern Dance', and my all-time favourite female muse. Her teachings tell us that anything going on inside our body is shown on the outside.

The Graham Technique was developed to evoke in the dancers, and the audience alike, a heightened awareness of life. Usually the characters of her works divided into two complementary parts representing the two aspects of the human psyche – good and bad, yin and yang.

I'm almost certain you are aware of your posture. Most people are because we are taught it from an early age "Sit up straight" "Stop slouching" "Shoulders back". But rarely do people know why good posture is so important. Nor do people truly know what good posture is. I've often been surprised to see clients stand super tall like a Queen's Guard and say to me "I know I'm supposed to stand like this, but I can't move properly!" Hmmm… well that's because you're not stood in correct posture for you.

Everybody is made the same. We each have a head, a spine, legs, arms, and skin. We all move in a similar fashion. But we all have our own style, our own unique way.

So if correct posture was to stand super straight with no flexibility of movement, then we'd all be pretty dull, in my opinion. Our good and bad would be neutralised, our yin and yang would need a boost. No offence to the Queen's Guards, I'm only using them for example, of course.

Your waist line divides your body into upper and lower regions. Of course you know that. Your lumbar back (lower region) helps to stabilise your body's balance, and gives your body mobility in bending forwards, sideways and to a small extent backwards. You know that also.

But are you fully aware of the small muscles of your lumbar back which are vitally important to your powerful posture?

Your lumbar back is located between your lowest ribs and your tailbone. It is built for powerful and flexible movement. The four main muscles integral to smooth lumbar region actions are:

Multifidus: The largest and most central of your deep lumbar back muscles. Its fibers branch to connect between each vertebrae of your lower spine, giving stability to your lower back, especially during movement.

Levator Ani: Three small muscles between your tailbone and pelvis. Each one extends your spine; pulls your tailbone forward to open and support your vertebrae and assists your waist in resisting increased pressure during coughing, vomiting and going to the loo.

Quadratus Lumborum: Two wide rectangular deep muscles either side of your spine that attach your 12th ribs to your pelvis. These are massively important for your waists' stability, especially when breathing in.

Psoas: A long muscle that splits from your middle spine, over both hips and down the front of your groin on both sides. It plays a huge part in keeping your hip bones pointing forward.

Good posture in your lumbar back initiates the presence of the three natural curves in your spine. The first natural curve is at your neck, the second is in the middle of your spine and the third is in your lumbar region. By opening up the three natural curves in your spine, you are distributing your body weight evenly; taking pressure off your vertebral discs and aiding your nerve impulses in the somatic nervous system and the autonomic nervous system. Don't worry if you're unfamiliar with the nervous system, I'll give you a rundown of it shortly.

Opening up your lumbar spine ensures that your hips are placed in alignment with your pubic bone, and your psoas muscle is adequately supporting your pelvis for pain free hip flexion such as walking, bending and sitting.

So how do you get good lumbar back posture without looking like a Queen's Guard?

Imagine you have a torch light on each hip bone. The light beams must be directed forward. Now, when I asked Denise to shine her beams forward, she instantly stuck her pubic bone out and tucked her bottom under. Yes, this action emphasizes the hip bones, but it also shortens the psoas muscle and bulks the front thighs which creates stiff and restricted movement.

I then asked Denise to imagine she had a light beam on her pubic bone, just at the front of her vagina. The beam should be directed forward to create a triangle of light beams. Two lights at her hips and one light on her vagina.

Instantly Denise's posture became easy, comfortable and free. She told me she felt no pain. Instantly. She said she felt "weirdly taller". She also said she felt in control, "like I could glide".

'Tilting your pelvis in-line' is one of the 'Feel Alive System' principles to powerful posture and you should practise this principle every day whenever possible.

Experience Your Beam

A Daily Reminder to Practise Your Pelvic Tilt

Take a minute out now to try adjusting your lumbar posture… Stand up with your feet hip distance apart, your toes pointing forward and your heels in line with your toes. Now, actively lift your knee caps. I don't mean lift your foot off the ground. Keep your feet planted into the floor. I mean pull your knee caps up to engage your thigh muscles. This has nothing to do with your lower back posture, but it does give you a good strong standing position to hold yourself with your knees supported but not 'snapped' super straight.

Feel relaxed in your legs. Place your hands on your hips and wiggle your bum a little, just to feel alive in your pelvis area. Okay, now relax your hips and feel your pelvis rest. From here, tilt your pelvis forward to tuck your bum under so your pubic bone sticks out. Reverse this movement so now your bum is sticking out. Now bring your pelvis back to the center.

Keep your knees supported by lifting your knee caps to engage your thigh muscles. Take a deep breath in. Fill your lungs and feel the air lift your body taller.

Begin an exhale. As you breathe out, feel yourself lifting your weight out of your hips. Imagine your tailbone lengthening to open your lower back vertebrae. Take a mental note of where your pelvis rests. Are you resting with your tailbone tucked under or sticking out? This tilt will be tiny and you may not notice it at first. Take a few moments to let your mind focus on your pelvis area.

Keep the lift in your lower body and keep breathing. It's funny how people hold their breath when focusing on their posture.

Now, imagine a plumb line from your tailbone down to the floor. I'd like you to tilt your tailbone (not your hips) so that the plumb line is directly dropping down between your two parallel feet, just between your ankle bones. Close your eyes if you feel this would help.

Keep your knees supported by lifting your knee caps to engage your thigh muscles. You will notice when you consciously do this that your knees push back. Try to not let that happen. Keep pulling up to take the pressure out of your knees.

You should now feel longer with space between the vertebrae in your lower back. The front of your hips (your psoas muscle) should feel flatter and your hips should be aligned with your pubic bone pointing forwards.

Don't worry if you don't feel this straight away. As in any task, it takes practise. Watch yourself in a mirror, or window reflection, and keep practising at any time of the day: whilst shopping, whilst cooking or while performing any routine standing task. Gradually you will become aware of the positioning of your lower back.

This is where your first journal task begins. I would like you to write a few lines explaining what you have experienced. This doesn't need to be award winning writing, just make it note form. This journal is for you to reflect on during your journey to powerful posture. Over the years, clients have often remarked that their journal has been a source of motivation to become more aware of their body and appreciate how much they didn't know!

Date	Power Posture	Awareness	Notes
30th January	Tilt Pelvis	Noticed I sit in my lower back.	When I lift my weight out of my hips with a breath in, I feel so much taller. Today I have practised my posture when standing and sitting. I noticed after a few minutes though that I forgot about my posture and then noticed I have gone back to my original sink into my hips.
31st January	Tilt Pelvis	Interestingly, I noticed my posture this morning when I was looking in the bathroom mirror.	I corrected my posture at the bathroom mirror and was amazed to see the difference in my bum! Yesterday I felt the difference, but today I saw it. Wow!

How wonderful the gift of writing is, eh!? Once you have written your notes, take a moment to try the same movement while sitting.

Sit at the edge of your chair or bed or wherever you are comfortable. Place your feet hip distance apart with your toes pointing forward. Breathe in to feel the air open your spine vertebrae. Breathe out and keep the lift.

Rock your pelvis forward slightly so you can feel your weight on your sitting bones. Imagine the plumb line through your lower spine down through your tailbone and into the seat you are sat on.

Place your hands on your knees. Just relaxed, but make sure your fingers are prepared for supporting your weight because you're going to be moving your weight off balance.

Breathe in, feeling tall just as you did when you were standing. Breathe out and roll your sitting bones forward and backward.

Breathe in to return to the centre line where your tailbone is long through your lower back. Feel your sitting bones in the centre.

What do you notice about your lower back sitting posture? It's not a massive revelation that you will encounter, but hopefully you will notice that you don't only need to stand to have powerful posture. Sitting and laying down are positions where you can consciously change the way your spine is held.

Take a few moments to notice your new sitting position, where do you hold your weight when sitting? Do you tilt your pelvis, sinking your weight into your hips and shortening your lumbar vertebrae?

Or do you lean forward slightly, sticking your bottom out which over stretches your lower back muscles? Write what you notice in your notebook.

Remember to imagine light beams from your pubic bone and both hips. These lights create a triangle. If you're sitting with incorrect posture, your pubic bone light beam has disappeared because your weight has tilted forward and your light is directed downward. With effortless powerful sitting posture, your pubic bone light should be directed forward and your weight should be in alignment with your tailbone down to the floor. Just like a toddler sits, with a straight spine. Remember to keep your spine straight but with a relaxed pelvis.

Practise your lower back powerful posture every day. A great reminder of tilting your pelvis in-line is to imagine a plumb line from your tailbone down between your feet when opening the fridge door. I call this, quite simply, 'Fridge Door Tilt'.

So experience your Fridge Door Tilt daily. Each time you open the fridge door:

Lift your weight out of your hips by opening your lumbar vertebrae; center your spine; engage your thigh muscles by lifting your knee caps; and lengthen through your psoas muscle across the front of your hips. Your pubic bone light should be shining forward. Imagine a plumb line from your tailbone down between your parallel feet in-line with your ankle bones.

Remember to write any notes related to your posture in your notebook.

Energise Your Pelvic Tilt

Yin and Yang With Wood

The first theory of Traditional Chinese Medicine is that all the systems that make up a human are in equal unity. The second is that all things are a result of the relationship of yin and yang. Both yin and yang must be in balance for your body to be in balance.

Yang is the good, light, active, hot, male element and represents heaven.

Yin is the bad, dark, passive, cold, female element and represents the underworld (earth).

Everyone is made up of both yin and yang elements; yin exists within yang, and yang exists within yin.

Yin is considered to be substance within the body – blood, air, hormones, food and waste.

Yang is considered to be action within the body – qi, life force, energy. Qi (yang) is the force within your body that counteracts gravity. It holds your vital organs in place and helps your body systems transport body substances (yin).

The Wu Xing, or more often referred to as the 5-element theory, or sometimes known as the Nei Ching, is an ancient complex Chinese health and wellbeing system which connects Tao, yin and yang, and the five elements.

'People who lived in woodlands embraced the spirit of the fish; whose endurance could protect them from the forest watershed during spring rainfall.'

Can you recall from the opening chapter the ancient Chinese Tao folktale where we learn yang is heaven and yin is earth? The Wu Xing teaches that in addition to heaven and earth, yin and yang subdivided into the five elements: wood, fire, earth, metal and water. Man, who is believed to be the product of heaven and earth by the interaction of yin and yang, also contains the five elements.

'Endurance Of The Fish' connects your lumbar muscles, your liver and gallbladder, and your nervous system with the element wood.

Wood is a strong element. Have you ever really noticed wood? It is constantly growing, changing, evolving. An old broken tree trunk can look rotten, but a carpenter can make that very same piece of wood appear brand new. That's the beauty of wood. Its energy is constantly in a process of rebirth. In TCM, wood is associated with the eyes. It is believed that healthy wood energy generates healthy eyes and an optimistic vision for the future.

I have an interesting question for you... how many times when you've been tired and your eyes have felt dry have you been truly fed up with your world? For me, many times. Isn't it interesting that there is often a connection of tired body and negative thoughts, don't you think? And for me, it usually occurs after I've over indulged in something; be it food, drink or even really happy occasions! When my liver and gallbladder are working super hard after excess, I know my wood element is in rebirth mode.

By being mindfully aware of the energy within your wood element and taking moments within your day to appreciate your own ever growing, changing and evolving energy within you, your body will positively respond. I'm not suggesting you run out into the open and hug a tree (unless you want to), but by abstractly connecting your flow of qi with the flow of the wood grain, you're assisting your liver's healthy functioning.

According to Traditional Chinese Medicine philosophy, the liver smooths the flow of qi in your body. Qi travels around your body as energy, but it's not the energy created from the metabolism of food, that's a different kind. Qi is a clear fluid which runs through each yin and yang meridian of your body just below your skin's surface, giving 'life force' to all organs. This smooth qi also nourishes your tendons and ligaments. It is the act of qi flowing smoothly around your body which connects all your vital organs with your body systems and creates harmonious element energy.

"The principle of yin and yang is the basis of the entire universe. It is the principle of everything in creation. It brings about the transformation to parenthood; it is the root and source of life and death." - Nei Ching.

Each vital organ in your body has a pair. One is a yin organ and the other is a yang organ. These 'pairs' are based on the meridian pathways and they are governed by one of the five elements. Each element works both as a generator and a controller to other elements.

Look at the Wu Xing diagram in 'The Wu Xing' chapter, or the one you copied into your notebook. You can see clearly the Wu Xing full circle effect where wood generates fire, fire generates earth, earth generates metal, metal generates water, and water generates wood. Round and round and round, the harmony goes full circle and your body and mind are both equally happy.

But if there is a failure to nourish; if there is a congestion in the smooth flow of qi, which could be when the body is weak, sick or injured, the related element rebels and over controls its opposite element by attacking it. This is a simple synopsis of a very complex system. So don't panic if you don't get it straight away, it takes Wu Xing students months to learn this. I'll try to explain it below.

Your wood energy is generated by your water energy; water feeds wood. However, if your earth energy has too much or too little yin or yang, from weakness, sickness or injury, it attacks your water energy; earth subjugates water.

Basically, a weak spleen (a yin organ) attacks the kidneys (another yin organ). As you can see in the Wu Xing Interactions diagram, the kidneys nourish the liver (also a yin organ), so now that the kidneys are weak, the liver receives less sustenance. Similarly for the yang organs; a weak stomach attacks the bladder which when 'happy' generates the gallbladder.

So do you see how everything is starting to connect to everything else?

Let's go back to Shanghai Pudong Airport for a moment. I've just finished my coffee and Denise has offered to take my rubbish to the bin.

"57 years old and already a geriatric! Car accident. 10 years ago though. Half my spleen was removed and now I suffer with terrible lower back pain. I'm so tired, my eye keeps bloody twitching."

Can you see why I smiled? Denise had a weak spleen and she was telling almost textbook symptoms of her yin deficiency: earth attacking water which manifested in affected wood energy; tiredness, eye problems and tendon and ligament pains in her lower back.

Before I tell you how Denise rectified her posture and created "energy beyond her dreams" to quote Denise, I'm going to quickly go through the functions of the liver, gallbladder and the nervous system. Not because I want to give you an anatomy and physiology class, but because it is important that you can connect the structure and functions of your body to your powerful posture.

It is easy to overlook the internal workings of your magical body when focusing on your posture, but do you know something, to create strong powerful posture and reduce ligament and tendon pains *and* give a boost to your qi's smooth flow, you really do need to be mindfully aware of your liver, gallbladder and nervous system.

Remember a few pages back I told you that each vital yin organ within your body works as a 'pair' with another vital yang organ?

Well, your liver is a vital yin organ which is paired with your gallbladder. Your liver is actually a massive organ and its main function is to filter toxins from your blood travelling from your digestive tract; and to continue the metabolism process by secreting bile, which happens to be stored in your gallbladder, a yang organ that is connected to your liver.

Your yin liver is a triangle wedge shape that sits to the right side of your body under your right breast, above your waist in the upper region. The base of your liver is situated in the top part of your lumbar region, where three tubes connect your liver to other organs. The first tube is the bile duct which drains bile to your intestines to assist in digestion processes; the second tube is the portal vein which brings nutrient rich blood from your intestines to your liver for absorption and detoxifying, and the third tube is the hepatic artery which brings oxygenated blood from your heart to your liver and gallbladder to keep them functioning.

So your liver and gallbladder work in a 'pair' and they both each play an active role in the process of digestion through the production and storage of bile. The liver plays one extra vital role. It absorbs and releases glucose which is majorly important for giving your body energy; keeping the zing in your step, the sparkle in your eyes and an elevated and invigorated emotional mood: your smooth qi.

This is where your nervous system comes into play. Your liver cannot control the glucose levels within your blood without the close assistance of your nervous system.

The nervous system is your body's 'control centre'. It is responsible for sensing changes outside and within your body.

It makes decisions on how to react to the changes and controls all mental and emotional responses. Your nervous system works closely with your endocrine system to regulate body processes and also works closely with your digestive system to convert glycogen to glucose, your zing and sparkle elixir.

The nervous system is a large network of nerve cells and fibres that run down your spine from your brain and branch off to send nerve impulses to all parts of your body. It's a bit like a telecommunications centre; an organized chaos of messages.

Your central nervous system is the main communication system between what your eyes see in the outside world, the electrical impulses sent to your brain telling your body what you are experiencing and then the responses your body makes by sending messages along your spinal cord to the relevant body parts. As you probably know, your spinal cord is a long chain of nerve fibres and cells which runs from your brain through the bony parts of your spine and branches at your lumbar region into nerve roots.

The nervous system has two main parts:

The central nervous system (CNS) - your body's main communication system which consists of your brain and spinal cord.

The peripheral nervous system (PNS) which contains all the nerves outside of your central nervous system.

Your peripheral nervous system is subdivided into two parts:

The somatic nervous system (SNS) which contains 31 pairs of spinal nerves and 12 pairs of nerves originating from your brain; both govern impulses to your skeletal muscles.

The autonomic nervous system (ANS) which controls the automatic body activities of smooth muscle, cardiac muscle and the activities of glands.

Your autonomic nervous system is divided into two:

The sympathetic system which prepares your body for expending energy and deals with emergency situations.

The parasympathetic system which conserves energy and creates the conditions necessary for rest and sleep.

The way you hold your lower back has a huge influence on your nerve responses. When you have good posture the communication through your nervous system is quick and effortless – your body stays in control and efficiently sends electric impulses around your body.

But think about the hassle that is involved in transporting important messages when the pathway is not clear, due to obstructions of nerve roots, herniated discs or highly active pain receptors. It takes much more effort, and time. This creates a slower response which causes your body's other systems to slow down such as the circulatory system with reduced blood flow, the respiratory system with shallow breathing and your digestive system with slower bile production and secretion.

A fab little exercise I used to do with my friends at university when studying anatomy and physiology was to people watch and analyse their posture. I call it a 'Body Scan'. It is a really interesting exercise to do to quickly become aware of good and not so good postures. When you get chance, take a moment to casually observe someone and imagine the positioning of their liver and gallbladder. As you look at them, visualize the bigger part of their right triangle shaped liver sitting on your left side. Imagine their gallbladder just behind and attached to their liver on your right side.

Can you see in your mind's eye just how massive their liver is? And as you visualise their liver, imagine its weight!

Follow your eye line down to their waist and imagine the three tubes branching off their liver on your left side. Can you see how close the tubes are to their waist area and lumbar region? Imagine the three tubes as the person moves. Do you imagine the tubes are stretched or squashed?

Now look at the person's lower back posture. Do you notice their tailbone – is it tucked under, sticking out or in-line? In your mind's eye connect the three tubes of their liver and gallbladder with the central nervous system's nerve roots in their lumbar region and their tailbone positioning. Do you imagine a clear pathway between them? Can you start to see how their posture influences the efficiency and ease of the organs and systems?

Incorrect lumbar posture affects your nervous system and the stability and strength of your spine. Overtime, the weak muscles reduce the smooth flow of qi around your body which reduces your body's ability to support your internal organs and leads to slumped waist support. If the slumped posture is not corrected, it is possible, and likely, to lead to liver congestion and bile duct, portal vein or hepatic artery obstruction. The consequence is weak wood energy showing as tiredness, eye problems, tendon and ligament aches and pains and reduced detoxing of waste materials in the blood.

So how did Denise rectify her symptoms of liver weakness within six weeks to gain "energy beyond her dreams"?

It was simple really... she started watching people, she transferred what she had noticed in people's postures into her own posture, she wrote notes in her journal, she performed the Fridge Door Tilt daily reminder and she became mindful of her lumbar region weakness. I spoke with Denise every Wednesday morning to discuss what she had noticed in her body as she was becoming more aware of how everything is connected.

Also, I showed her easy and effective 10-minute morning movements that stretch, strengthen and support her lumbar region muscles. Do you know what the best thing about this morning routine is... it is done in bed! So Denise didn't say she didn't have time, because it happened so easily.

"I woke up, I stretched in bed, I lifted my legs for a bit, I laid in bed for a minute more and then I jumped out of bed. And I can honestly say I didn't even think about it after a few days, I just did it. Like making a cup of tea, it became second nature."

Execute Your Pelvic Tilt

'Pillow Pilates' Lumbar Spine Morning Movement

Here is one of the exercises that Denise performed each morning. I have broken 'Lateral Leg Lift' down into straight forward, jargon free instructions.

I go through this exercise and 23 others in much more detail in my 'Feel Alive 6-Week Online Program', which I give information about at the back of this book.

Below are the instructions for Lateral Leg Lift Abduction and Lateral Leg Lift Adduction. Simple reminder instructions for you to copy if you feel following these instructions is too detailed, are in the 'What Next?' chapter. The instructions below here are for you to fully understand the movements and breath work involved:

Lay on your mattress. It doesn't really matter which direction you are, length ways or width ways, as long as you have enough room to fully stretch your body from head to toe.

Lay on your right side with your lower arm (your right arm) under your head and stretching in the opposite direction to your feet.

Your top arm (your left arm) should rest in front of your chest with your palm facing down, for support against wobbling. If you feel uncomfortable in your neck area, place a pillow between your arm and ear to support the weight of your head.

Make sure your hips and shoulders are vertically stacked, one on top of the other with no leaning or sway, and make sure your shoulders are back, so your chest is proud. Your waist should be strong by sucking your belly button into your spine and lengthened by pulling tall through the crown of your head – you should easily be able to put the fingers of your supporting hand through the space you have created under your lowest rib. I like to call this your 'diamond waist'.

Now, the important part of this preparation is to engage your beams! Make sure your hips and pubic bone (your triangle) are in alignment and you are lengthening your tailbone down towards your feet. Shine your beams from your pelvis (your hips and pubic bone) forward.

Take a deep breath in to lift your top leg (left leg) to hip level (6-8 inches), actively reaching through your toes. This is working your outer thigh, your abductor muscle, and predominantly your lumbar region muscles: multifidus, levator ani, quadratis lumborum and psoas. Breathe out to lower your leg back down to meet your right leg, keeping your 'diamond waist'.

Repeat 10 times.

ATTENTION: Take notice of your top shoulder. DO NOT allow your shoulder to roll forward or creep up to your ear. Actively lengthen through your neck and keep your chest open.

After the 10th lift of your left leg, keep your left leg lifted at hip height (approximately 6-8 inches off the mattress) and take another breath in while lifting your right leg to meet your left leg. This is working your inner thigh, your adductor muscle.

Breathe out to lower both legs down to the mattress, keeping your diamond waist engaged and the length through your spine from your tailbone up to the crown of your head.

Inhale to lift your left leg, breathe in again to lift your right leg. Take a long breath out to lower both your legs (which should squeeze together) down to the mattress.

ATTENTION: Take notice of the effort required to lift your bottom leg. Make sure to lengthen through your waist and extend energy through your lower arm and fingers. Keep the length through your neck and keep your top shoulder down away from your ear.

Repeat 10 times.

Roll over and repeat the whole routine laying on your left side.

So you are lengthening through your spine from your tailbone up to the crown of your head. Your shoulders are back and you are strengthening your waist by sucking your belly button into your spine.

Tilt your pelvis so your hips and pubic bone are in alignment and your 'beams' are shining! Lengthen your tailbone in-line with your feet and squeeze your bum to support the position.

Breathe in to lift your right leg up to hip level (6-8 inches off the mattress), and breathe out to lower your right leg down. Keep lengthening your spine.

After 10 repetitions, keep your right leg lifted. Take another inhale to lift your left leg to meet your right leg (keeping long through your spine and neck, and using your right hand in front of your chest to support your weight from tilting or falling off balance), breathe out to lower both legs back down to the mattress.

Repeat 10 times. To finish, hug your knees into your chest.

'Endurance Of The Fish' works your lumbar muscles; strengthening your hips and lower back, correcting poor lumbar spine posture to open the meridian channels to your nervous system, which then stimulates your liver and gallbladder boosting the flow of your body's qi and creating sparkling energy.

Denise found as she performed these two exercises, that if she focused her mind on the yin and yang relationship with the interrelationship of the ever changing wood element, she could really start to notice a shift in her mood - she noticed she was feeling less tired.

She told me, after our second lesson, that during the week she had felt 'royally miffed off'. She didn't know why, she just felt irritated by the whole world. And so she took herself off to bed. While she was laying in bed, she began thinking about her tired mood and how she had learnt from Traditional Chinese Medicine theory that weakness in her liver is connected to irritability - when qi is not flowing smoothly, the blockage in her liver shows as tiredness.

After a short moment of sulking, Denise started performing the lateral leg lift movements and instantly began enjoying the harmonious energy she was opening within her liver and gallbladder meridians, along with the gorgeous lower back posture she was strengthening.

Denise now continues to practise the Lateral Leg Lift Series as part of her everyday morning routine. Although she completed the 'Feel Alive 6-Week Program' a while ago, we do keep in touch and she tells me she would not consider stopping her 10 minutes morning Pilates routine.

"10 years ago I had a severe car accident which affected my body and in particular my lower back. Until a couple of months ago my lower back was aching, painful and stiff. By learning Pilates and the Traditional Chinese Medicine philosophy with Jessica, I managed to get rid of all of this within a very short amount of time. Now I am able to do it fully independently. I can't imagine what my retired life would've been like... I can only think back to the torture of the pain I experienced and wish to never return to that point again. I am now consciously aware of my lower back posture, which has had a huge impact on my energy levels - I seriously now have energy beyond my dreams! That is the reason why I shall continue practising my morning routines, and the big reason why I recommend the Feel Alive 6-Week Program to anyone who feels they need encouragement and motivation to become fully aware of their body."

Breath Of The Bird

Embrace Your Yin and Yang for Life Enhancing Jing

Connecting your heart and small intestine

with your latissimus dorsi muscle and cardiovascular system

to the fire element for renewing and preserving your

life enhancing energy.

"Never slouch, as doing so compresses the lungs,

overcrowds other vital organs,

rounds the back and throws you off balance."

- Joseph Pilates

Engage What You've Got

Principle of Upper Region Powerful Posture

"Never slouch" Joseph Pilates is the father of the Pilates Contrology exercise method, and my favourite male in the performing arts world. He began his life in 1883 as a frail, sickly child. With his strong attitude towards 'fixing his health problems', he started learning martial arts and yoga. In late 1912 he left his home country, Germany, as a fit and strong young man to become a circus artist in Britain. At the outbreak of World War I he was captured by British authorities and held at a camp on the Isle of Man. It was during this time that he combined his knowledge and understanding of the human body, martial arts and yoga to help injured, sick and weak inmates return to health. His genius was in using everyday items to assist in the process. He used mattress springs to aid in resistance for slow and deliberate muscle strengthening exercises, and he used chairs to assist in reclining support for lengthening limbs and upper body stretches.

After the war, he immigrated to New York, USA, where he met his wife Clara and began his legacy of working with dancers, such as Martha Graham, to rehabilitate injuries and build suppleness and strength without bulking muscles.

"Never slouch, as doing so compresses the lungs, overcrowds other vital organs, rounds the back, and throws you off balance." - Joseph Pilates.

'Well when it is said like that, doesn't it make sense? Of course slouching rounds my back. Yes, indeed it does throw me off balance when I'm walking and looking at my feet. Umm... yes, when I think about it, I can understand my vital organs are compressed and overcrowded when I'm rounding my back and not paying attention to my posture. But it's uncomfortable when I don't slouch, and I feel like a right idiot sticking my chest out like a peacock.' Is that what goes through your mind when you're reminded to 'draw your shoulders back'? You are not at all alone on that thought.

When people start training with me, I often spend the first session focusing on the latissimus dorsi muscle. This is the king of all muscles when correcting posture and, when engaged in your powerful posture, allows your chest to be proud without 'sticking your boobs out'. Ladies, this principle is brilliant if you slouch to hide a large bosom.

Your latissimus dorsi (lats) is a large wide sheet of muscle that starts at the back of your shoulders, under your armpits. The fibres run diagonally towards your spine and attach into the vertebrae of your waist and lumbar region.

By engaging your lats you are correctly pulling your shoulders back and down into your spine, without 'sticking your chest out' or feeling uncomfortable. You are actually engaging your sides, back and chest to open your upper body region, creating natural internal space and reducing pressure on your vital organs from your heart right down to your intestines (you'll learn about this in the 'Energise' section of this chapter).

For optimal results from your powerful posture, it is really important that you understand how to engage the lats:

Start by pulling tall through the crown of your head and lengthen your tailbone away. Slide your shoulder blades down your back and feel proud in your chest.

The best way I describe this is by imagining you have a torch light in the gap at the front of your collar bone - your clavicle. The beam of light should shine forward. If you are sticking your chest out, the light beam directs up, and similarly if you are heavy in your ribs the light beam is directed down. Make sure to engage your lumbar spine powerful posture: let your beams shine forward from your lumbar posture (your hip bones and pubic bone) and from your thoracic posture (your chest).

Now, cross your arms over your chest and cup your armpits with your hands. Use one hand if you feel uncomfortable. Cough. Not a meek, shy cough but a proper meaningful cough.

Do you feel your armpit hollow and the underneath become stronger? Well, that is the top of your latissimus dorsi engaging.

Now try engaging the muscle with your arms by your sides. Don't worry if you do not feel your latissimus dorsi engage straight away - it does take time. And once you've got it, you've got it!

When I'm showing people how to engage their lats for the first time, I ask them to place their fingers with a firm pressure under my armpits and feel the difference when I engage my lats. This is helpful for sensing where and how strong the latissimus dorsi muscle is.

Have a go... wrap your fingers around someone's armpits. Of course your fingers do not need to be directly in their armpit, just slightly behind. You'll know you've got it when the person laughs or coughs because you'll feel the muscle. It is like a cobra snake's expandable hood. Once you can feel where the muscle is on someone else, you'll have better control when you engage your own.

'Draw your shoulders back' is one of the 'Feel Alive System' principles to powerful posture, and you should practise this principle every day whenever possible.

Experience What You've Got

A Daily Reminder for Drawing Your Shoulders Back

Rounding of the upper back is known in therapy work as 'Hyperkyphosis'. It is an increase in the middle spine (thoracic) natural curve, with both shoulders rolling forward and consequently the head jutting forward.

In the 'Endurance Of The Fish' chapter, I introduced 'people watching' to you, where you body scan peoples posture and their internal organs to evaluate your awareness of correct posture. Let's now take that awareness to the next level.

By looking at a person in standing, you can determine how they feel, what injuries they may have or had in the past and areas of the body which may cause problems in the future. Postural assessments can be done on yourself also, but you'll need help from a good friend or family member, one who you are not shy around - you'll need to let your ego go and be naturally normal.

Here's how to do a 'Postural Assessment' on yourself:

You should dress in clothes that allow for clear observation – your underwear is ideal, but tight clothes are also good if you feel a little uncomfortable having your photograph taken in your frilly pants!

Stand comfortably with your feet hip distance apart, your arms by your sides and your eye line looking forward.

Ask a good friend or a family member to take a full body photograph of your left side, in a standing position, your right side, again in a standing position, and from the front and finally from the back, both also in a standing position.

Now is the cringe moment - you need to analyse your posture in each photograph.

Start with your feet - see if they are turned in or turned out. Look at your ankles, are they equal thickness? Compare the bulk of your calves (lower legs), hamstrings (back of thighs), quadriceps (front of thighs) and gluteal muscles (bottom). Is one side predominantly bigger than the other? Do both knees face forward, and are they at the same level? Are your hips aligned - is one side forward or does one side sit higher than the other?

Look at your hands - where is the position of each one next to your thighs - are your fingers resting at the same place on both sides? Follow your spine curves, does any area look exaggerated? Pay close attention to your lumbar spine - can you see your beams (in your imagination, of course) with a plumb line from your tailbone down to the heels of your feet? Are your shoulders rolling forward - can you imagine your latissimus dorsi muscle drawing your shoulders back so your thoracic light beam is shining forward or is your chest slouched down with your head jutting forward and your light beam shining down? What about the opposite - is your head too far back?

Now look at your side profile photograph only. Draw an imaginary line from your ear, through the centre of your shoulder, through the centre of your hip joint, down your leg through your knee and ankle bone (make sure your line goes through the bone that sticks out and not the top of your foot).

Is the line straight? From this line you can see if your body weight is heavy in your natural curves and you can assess where you need to lengthen taller through your height.

A posture assessment on yourself can be tough on your ego, so be kind to yourself. You are an amazing creature. Embrace looking at your body and allow yourself to feel proud for identifying where weaknesses are within your body.

Once you have observed your posture from your photographs, write your findings in your journal. Or draw an outline of a human shape from the side, the front and the back and label the areas of weakness. Make sure to put the date on your journal page because I do recommend you do this assessment every three months or so, to observe your postural improvements.

Make a note in your posture assessment page of where your body is weak. Weakness is shown as being out of alignment. For example, in hyperkyphosis the shoulders are rounded, the chin sticks out further than the collar bones and the knees are slightly bent - usually one side more than the other.

Muscles that are short and tight need releasing or stretching. In this case the chest muscles (pecs) need stretching. Muscles that are lengthened and weak need strengthening. In this case the latissimus dorsi (lats) need strengthening.

In today's technological world (driving, computers, smart phones) it has become common for people to have a mild form of hyperkyphosis where weakness in their upper body muscles (lengthening in their latissimus dorsi and shortness in their pectorals) creates poor posture in their upper body: their chest becomes heavy, their shoulders slouch and their head juts forward. The space within their ribs reduces and their breathing becomes shallower. This shorter breath creates tension around the shoulders, which doesn't help their already poor posture.

BUT... by strengthening the latissimus dorsi muscle, the chest is released and stretched creating a proud pectoral area and strong balanced shoulders. A great daily reminder of engaging your latissimus dorsi muscle is to draw your shoulders back in the shower.

Here's how:

Start by engaging your lumbar region powerful posture, pull tall through your waist to take the weight out of your hips. Take a deep breath in while squeezing your shoulders back. Imagine pulling your shoulder blades as far back as possible so you could hold a coin between the two. Make sure to keep your ears in line with your shoulders - don't let your head push forward.

Exhale to return to your normal posture. Breathe in to lift your shoulders up to your ears, and breathe out to drop your shoulders down, allowing any tension to release from your upper body region.

Now, remembering what you have learnt from 'Endurance Of The Fish', keep your powerful lumbar posture and your lumbar beams engaged. Breathe in to feel tall through your waist. As you breathe out squeeze your latissimus dorsi muscle down, feeling your armpits and the muscles across the top of your breasts engage. Repeat several times, breathing in to feel tall through your neck and imagine your light beam shining from your collar bone.

Each time you take a shower, where you are in your own private space and you can take a really good stretch through your chest without feeling too self-conscious, experience engaging your latissimus dorsi muscle.

Start by tilting your tailbone in-line. Take a deep breath in, and as you exhale draw your shoulders down into your back. Feel your lats engage and the pectorals across the front of your chest stretch.

Make sure to lift your chest proud by imagining a light beam from your collar bone. The light should shine forward, not down or up. And remember to write any observations related to your powerful posture in your journal notebook.

Powerful posture in your upper body region is so much more important for your body than 'looking good'. Let me illustrate to you how by telling you about Valerie...

Energise Your Shoulders

Yin and Yang With Fire

A few years ago I met a lady, Valerie, at a health and wellness seminar in the UK. I was hosting a table in the holistic therapy suite. Valerie was attending the seminar for research into her restless legs symptoms. We chatted in a consultation style conversation and I rapidly began to understand where her problems were rooted.

Valerie was a young 68 year old. She had been married to Roger for 19 years (both on their second marriage) and they had a very loving relationship.

Unfortunately, Valerie's restless legs had meant that she and Roger slept in separate rooms, which was upsetting for both of them and caused disagreements and unhappiness.

Valerie had initially approached me as a holistic massage therapist, hoping that I could relax her muscles so she could remedy her night leg twitches and quickly return to her and Roger's slumber room. But during our consultation, I could see that massage would not benefit her as she was.

You see, she had terribly heavy shoulders. Although she complained to me of experiencing daily headaches and brain fog (and also informed me that it takes her at least two cups of coffee and a puff on her e-cig to get going in the morning) I do mean she had very heavy shoulders in the literal sense.

Valerie had what is known as 'a postural slouch'. She had large breasts and she hid them well. She told me her chest had started to develop before puberty, and because of her childhood embarrassment, her shoulders had rolled forward in an attempt to hide her rapidly growing breasts. Over time, this slouch had consciously become a habit and had unconsciously caused massive internal cardiovascular issues.

The Traditional Chinese Medicine perspective of restless leg syndrome is that a disruption to the jing energy restricts the flow of nutrient rich blood to the legs. The main organs associated with the cardiovascular system, the flow of blood, are: the heart, a yin organ, and the small intestine, a yang organ. These two organs are associated with the element fire which is connected to pre-puberty and the mental quality of passion (strong emotions).

Let's get technical for a short moment, because it is important that you can see in your minds' eye the functioning of your cardiovascular system for you to understand the connections that lead to Valerie's restless legs.

Your yin heart sits in your thoracic cavity between your two lungs, above your diaphragm. It needs space to expand before it contracts to pump your yin blood around your body.

Now, imagine you can see when assessing your posture from the photographs taken by your good friend, that your upper body is slouched - your shoulders roll forward, your back is rounded and your ribs drop down into your waist area.

Can you visualise where your heart sits in relation to your two lungs and your diaphragm? Instead of having space to expand freely, as it does when you have a tall powerful posture, your heart is squashed between your two lungs and diaphragm and it has to work hard to expand in order to pump your yin blood to other vital organs.

As I'm sure you know, any muscle grows in size when it is exercised, and the heart is no different. Due to the intense hard work the heart endures to push into the small space, the muscle wall becomes thicker. BUT the wall grows internally, therefore reducing the area within your heart, lowering the amount of flowing yin substance and increasing your blood pressure. I imagine the squashed heart pumping is a bit like trying to bake a cake with a lid on the tin... although it pushes the surrounding obstacles, the mixture inside cannot rise and so the cake's content becomes heavy and thick.

In TCM, each yin organ is paired with a yang organ, and the heart's yang organ is the small intestine. The heart pumps oxygenated blood to the small intestine where it becomes nutrient rich with jing.

I'll tell you a little bit about jing before I explain the connections of the heart, small intestine and blood.

Jing is the body's essence for energy. It is a yin substance. We humans are born with a 'pre-natal' jing. That is to say that our parents, on our conception, give us a fund of jing. This essence is stored in our kidneys. It stays in our kidneys throughout our lifetime, and is gradually used when our body is desperate for a boost; such as in times of stress, illness, and over indulgence of sexual activity, drinking or smoking.

Each time our body uses our pre-natal jing, manifestations of aging begin to appear such as stiffness of joints, back ache, knee pain, aching bones and tendons, poor memory, weak eyesight, changes in the skin and weaker pulse, which incidentally is a factor of brain fog and headaches.

Once our pre-natal jing is consumed we die. I'm sorry to say it quite so bluntly, but it is quite literally as simple as that!

Post-natal jing is acquired through metabolising food and drink and is nourished with exercise and meditation. Jing feeds the body with energy. When yin and yang is balanced in the body, there is no need to deplete the pre-natal kidney jing funds because we get enough energy from our post-natal jing.

Jing (the body's essence) is used every day for fuelling the body's efficient functions, such as breathing, pumping blood, digesting food, excreting waste products, and enabling our fully functioning senses.

Keep in mind that all living creatures are made up of yin and yang. Qi is life force and it is a yang action. Jing is life essence and is a yin substance. The two must be equally balanced for the body to emanate a glowing shine of health and wellness.

So let's now look at the Traditional Chinese Medicine Wu Xing Interactions diagram in 'The Wu Xing' chapter to understand the responsibility of the fire element.

When your qi and jing are in balance, your heart and small intestine are generated by your liver and gallbladder (wood), which are generated by your kidneys and urinary bladder (water). Your kidneys and urinary bladder are nourished by your lungs and large intestine (metal) which are cared for by your stomach and spleen (earth). Your stomach and spleen are generated by your heart and small intestine (fire). The harmony goes full circle.

Now, when your qi and jing are not balanced, for example when your heart is not given a boost of qi energy from your liver; your cardiovascular system attacks the respiratory system: your lungs and large intestine (metal). Your lungs and large intestine are now in disharmony with your stomach and spleen (earth) and attack the nervous system: your liver and gallbladder (wood).

Your nervous system then attacks the digestive system: your stomach and spleen (earth), which then attacks the urinary system: your kidneys and urinary bladder (water). Do you remember that pre-natal jing, your essential energy for life, is stored in the kidneys?

When qi and jing are in disharmony, the kidneys cannot nourish the liver because the water element is putting the majority of its energy into controlling the fire element. In TCM, fire is associated with strength and warmth, impatience and restlessness. And when the fire element is weak, these emotions go into overdrive!

So, can you now start to see the pattern... if the flow of qi surrounding the heart is obstructed, then the heart fire element stops nourishing the spleen and stomach (earth element). The earth element then attacks the water element: the kidneys and urinary bladder. The kidneys are then yin deficient and the urinary bladder is yang strong.

It is believed in TCM that an excess of yang over yin within paired organs results in restlessness, high energy and agitation in the lower extremities. The body now needs a boost of pre-natal kidney jing in order to balance the yin and yang within the kidneys and urinary bladder.

But of course, we don't really want to be depleting our pre-natal kidney jing because we want to feel vibrant and alive, not stiff, aching and looking old! So we need to open the meridians of our vital organs to allow the jing energy to feed our body efficiently. In Valerie's case it was opening her meridian to her heart and small intestine, her fire element, by correcting her posture.

'Breath Of The Bird' connects your latissimus dorsi muscle with your heart and small intestine, opening up the meridian in your thoracic spine to allow your fire element to work with soft love and calm passion.

Execute Drawing Your Shoulders Back

'Pillow Pilates' Thoracic Spine Morning Movement

A good question you might be asking is 'How did Valerie heal herself?' Well, you know about Valerie's slouch in her upper body, and you know that during her pre-puberty age Valerie had become aware of her changing body and had adjusted her posture to hide her chest.

Over time, her curved posture had restricted the healthy functioning of her heart and the ability for her small intestine, her heart's yang organ, to absorb enough nutrients into her blood and transport the nutrient rich blood to her muscles for energy.

Valerie began practising the 'Breath Of The Bird' physical component, along with the other four principles of powerful posture, and within three weeks she began to feel a difference.

Often, Valerie praised 'Arm Circles' as being her favourite exercise for opening her chest, increasing mobility in her shoulders and strengthening her latissimus dorsi muscle.

Try 'Arm Circles' yourself, and remember to write notes in your journal reflecting how you feel before and after performing the movements. AND make sure to regularly record your posture changes in your posture assessment.

Simple reminder instructions, for you to copy if you feel following these instructions are too detailed, are at the back of this book in the 'What Now?' chapter. The instructions here are for you to fully understand the movements and breath work involved:

Sit tall at the edge of your mattress with your feet parallel on the floor and your powerful lumbar spine posture engaged. Your lumbar posture beams and your thoracic posture beam should be shining forward.

Inhale to stretch tall through your waist and lengthen through your neck area, making sure to tuck your chin in so you are long through the back of your neck.

Exhale to cross your arms and place your hands on each opposite hip. Keep your shoulders back with your chest proud. DO NOT let your shoulders roll forward.

Inhale to gently stroke your waist, bringing your arms up your body and over your head. Keep your shoulders down away from your ears.

Exhale to push both arms out to the sides, drawing a circular line down to your hips. Engage your lats to resist the movement - imagine pressing through water. Press both arms equally. DO NOT let one arm lead. And, of course, make sure to be pulling tall through your lumbar posture, while keeping your chest proud.

Repeat 10 times.

ATTENTION: Keep your beams shining forward at your collar bone and your hips and pubic bone, and squeeze your latissimus dorsi muscle down.

When the 'Breath Of The Bird Arm Circles' and the daily reminder of 'drawing your shoulders back in the shower' are practised each morning, strength is built in your latissimus dorsi muscle and you are stretching your chest area, where your heart and pericardium (a supportive sac surrounding your heart) sit.

When you engage and strengthen the latissimus dorsi muscle, qi energy nourishes the fire element in your cardiovascular system, boosting the blood flow to your small intestine where a higher measure of nutrients can be absorbed into your body. These nutrients transform into post-natal jing, which feeds your body all the essential energy it needs to stay looking and feeling young!

Remember, when qi and jing are in balance, the body rejoices with energy and alertness.

Alignment Of The Serpent

Embrace Your Yin and Yang to Energise Your Qi Reserves

Connecting your spleen and stomach

with your erector spinae muscles and digestive system

to the earth element for energising your qi reserves

and to de-stress.

"It's alright focusing on getting fit –

but if you don't understand your body;

your body doesn't understand you."

- Jessica Blackbond.

Engage Your Crown

Principle of Head to Tailbone Posture

In Traditional Chinese Medicine, it is said that "man must eat to absorb earth qi. The food essence [post-natal jing] transformed and transported through the stomach and spleen must be sent up to the lungs to combine with fresh air to produce the nutrients necessary for man's life activities." Therefore, the spleen is an important yin organ and the stomach is an important yang organ within the digestive system.

In Western medicine, the spleen is said to be connected to the lymphatic system and the body's immune system. Unlike Chinese medicine, there is no connection to the stomach and digestion. However, in recent years this difference in medical thought has begun to change and the Western medical thought is shifting closer in-line with TCM.

In TCM, it is said that the spleen is responsible for storing the body's excess qi. It is also directly linked to thoughts and emotions: a weak spleen creates worry and pensiveness, and excessive thinking and worrying can weaken the spleen.

Now, interestingly, both theories believe that your nervous system influences the actions of digestion by nerve impulses running down and up your spine.

Remember in 'Endurance Of The Fish', we saw Denise change her lumbar spine posture which opened up the blocked meridian in her nervous system to allow smooth flowing qi around her body? And in 'Breath Of The Bird' we saw Valerie straighten her thoracic spine which opened up her chest allowing her cardiovascular system to function well; allowing energy to efficiently fuel her body and preserve her pre-natal jing supply?

Well, in 'Alignment Of The Serpent' we will be looking at the posture of your cervical spine (base of the skull) and sacral spine (tailbone) to pull tall through the crown of your head down to your tailbone.

'Pulling tall through the crown of your head' is one of the 'Feel Alive System' principles to powerful posture, and refers to the length and alignment of your body in relation to qi and the pull of gravity. It also focuses on de-stressing your jing energy.

Stressed jing is a reference to a loss of pre-natal jing. In 'Breath Of The Bird', we looked at pre-natal jing and post-natal jing. To recap; jing is the energy essence of life. We are born with a pre-natal fund of jing energy, which is stored in our kidneys, and we acquire post-natal jing energy through metabolising food and water.

When we feel rundown, tired, ill, nervous, suffer with frequent colds, experience muscular aches and pains, battle with digestive issues... basically any 'energy' related ailment; our body uses our pre-natal jing energy to boost our wellbeing. The rundown symptoms we experience are a sign that we are stressing, and losing, our pre-natal jing energy.

To heal our body and renew vibrant health, we need to tune in to where we are losing our pre-natal jing. That is where the Wu Xing component comes in. As I said in Endurance Of The Fish, the Wu Xing is a complex system to understand, so don't worry if you do not get it just yet. The first step to vibrant health is to listen to your body, determine what your body is telling you, and establish balance in the area that has become weak. By following the exercises throughout this book, you will be doing just that.

Head to tailbone connection is important for the stability and mobility throughout your neck (cervical vertebrae), shoulders, chest and ribs (thoracic vertebrae), waist (lumbar vertebrae) and bottom (sacral vertebrae).

Basic knowledge of the human body tells us that all physical movement, including breathing, creates movement in the spine.

That makes sense. Of course the spine moves. So with an understanding of this knowledge, we can interpret that in a healthy, balanced body the erector spinae muscles (the muscles that run along each side of the spine) support and protect the alimentary canal (the digestive tract), which is a tube that runs in-front of your spinal column from your mouth all the way down and around your body to your bum; and the vital organs of the digestive system (the spleen and stomach) by moving the spine's vertebrae to absorb shock and distribute body weight evenly.

This movement occurs naturally when we walk, run, skip,

dance, wiggle, sit... when we move.

In Britain in the 1980's, there was a TV ad for Trebor Softmints. I always think about it when I'm teaching Alignment Of The Serpent because it showed a totally chilled out dude, made of pillows, walking, or rather rippling, down a 'pillow soft' street.

Mr Soft is an example of a person with weak erector spinae muscles. He lacks proper movement patterns. A person with weak movement patterns does not provide their body proper support and protection.

Imagine yourself walking with a long stride, and the movement rippling from your tailbone all the way up to your shoulders. To get the full 'chilled out' ripple you'd need to lean back slightly. Sometimes I love to be silly and walk like Mr Soft, but it hurts my back. I feel to be putting too much weight into my lower spine and really overworking my back muscles. I feel if I'm not careful I could cause damage to my spine's discs.

But some people do walk like Mr Soft. I see it regularly when I'm people watching. Okay, maybe not as exaggerated as I have just described, but you'll see what I mean when you're practising your people watching, and you'll know how to correct them!

As you learnt in 'Endurance Of The Fish' and 'Breath Of The Bird': the back is a complex area divided into two regions.

The occipital, the base of your skull, is an important part of your upper body region because it connects your spine to your head, stabilises your neck and allows the nervous system's communication to travel from your brain to the rest of your body.

A bit of general knowledge for you now: When you have a good massage, the occipital gets quite a lot of attention because it is the most common area of the body which holds a lot of stress and tension, and is one of the main causes of headaches and brain fog.

Each muscle group of your back attaches to multiple areas along your spine vertebrae. They function subconsciously and constantly to maintain the correct position of your head and spine in everyday movement, such as walking, sitting, dancing, standing etc. They co-ordinate with each other and take turns in shortening and tightening so that they do not tire under normal conditions.

The three groups of overlapping deep muscles integral to supporting the space between each vertebrae are:

Spinalis: The muscles most central to your spinal column. These muscles extend and rotate your head.

Longissimus: The 'in-betweeners'. These muscles rotate your head, extend your spinal column and bend your spine sideways.

Illiocostalis: The outside muscles. These muscles extend your spinal column and side bend your spine.

These hard working muscles are generally taken for granted unless they're injured, unhealthy or tense from stress. Hmmm... That's not right, is it? We should love our backs. We should show our back some appreciation.

Let's do it now by engaging a head to tailbone connection:

Stand or sit tall, with your tailbone in-line and beams shining, gently tilt your chin in towards your chest, open the base of your skull and draw your shoulders back (be chest proud by engaging your latissimus dorsi muscle, and don't forget to shine your beam from your collar bone).

Now, imagine you have string from the crown of your head down to your tailbone. The string is covered in beautifully shiny pearls. In order for your pearls to remain beautiful, each pearl must not touch its neighbouring pearl. To avoid any contact, the string needs to be pulled at each end: at the crown of your head and tailbone.

I'd like you to try pulling tall through the pearls from the crown of your head down to your tailbone now... Take a deep breath in through your nose to fill your lungs and allow the air to circulate your nasal passage.

Slowly breathe out through your mouth with a long "aaaahhhh". Let your voice sing. It's amazing how creating noise with your breath can deliver huge impact to your enlightened self-awareness.

As you exhale, release any tension from your neck. Of course this is easier said than done, but as I've said before: keep practising because you will get your lightbulb moment.

With your chin tilting towards your chest, create a lovely double chin, pull the string through the top of your head. Imagine the string is a plumb line down your neck - there is no slackening in the string because you are pulling the same plumb line at your tailbone.

Remember; you need to engage your thoracic powerful posture (chest proud) and your lumbar powerful posture (your pelvis triangle). Let each of your beams shine.

Inhale again and as you exhale, pull taller still so you are lifting your body weight up. Up. UP.   Imagine there is no limit to the lengthening of your spine.

How do you feel? Breathe in. Slowly breathe out and feel your body weight supported with a light body frame. This is how you can assist your qi to flow freely around your body with no obstruction or resistance.   Your qi will react so quickly to this action that you might go a little bit light headed. You may also be slightly surprised at how open and alert your mind becomes.

Take a moment to write a short journal note about how you feel when doing this 'Energy Stress Location Exercise'. Remember to put today's date and a short title outlining what you are doing. Make sure to include in your journal a note about your emotion. What mood do you feel before you move your spine vertebrae away from one another, creating length in your erector spinae muscles? Is your body feeling any symptoms of emotional stress - rundown, tired, ill, nervous, suffering with a cold, muscular aches and pains, digestive issues... ?

Write about any immediate experience you had when pulling tall through the crown of your head. As an example, many people experience a sense of alertness: their mind seems to 'switch on' with the lift through their spine.

Don't put too much effort into your writing, and certainly don't think about it too much. Your journal note doesn't need to be detailed, but it should be enough to tell your future self what you have just experienced. Remember to write the date and a short title, so you can recall the experience when you look back over your notes later.

'Pull tall through the crown of your head' is one of the 'Feel Alive System' principles to powerful posture. Practise the three principles, 'tilt your tailbone in line', 'draw your shoulders back', and 'pull tall through the crown of your head' as often as you can each day.

Experience Your Crown

A Daily Reminder to Pull Up Tall

How often do you make a cup of tea / coffee / drink / snack... anything that requires you to stand for a short while? I love tea, and when I'm at home I am often found in the kitchen boiling the kettle, standing super tall with my shoulders back and beams shining from my pelvis, ready to make my pot of Yorkshire Tea.

The next time you're boiling the kettle, take a few moments to pull the string of pearls at the crown of your head and at your tailbone. Remember to keep your eyes forward.   If you look down you're changing the position of your thoracic spine. You want to pull the crown of your head up.   It is similar to a deportment lesson, where you are balancing five hardback books on your head.

The difference here is that you are practising for comfort, not attitude. So you must breathe with your lift.

I remember when I first discovered how my breath was affecting my posture, which interestingly was affecting my moods. I was a Contrology Pilates Mat-Work student teacher. I'd just 'retired' from performing dance professionally and was in the middle of a very stressful time.

As a practical task at Pilates school, we students had to analyse one another's body in stillness. We were asked to work in pairs and just watch each other standing. Weird hey? But I'll tell you what... it was an extraordinary moment for me.

Josie was watching me. She was in her late 40's and was recovering from bladder prolapse surgery of which she told me was extremely successful in remedying her leaking when she laughed. I found that to be very fortunate because we spent the first five minutes of the task laughing - as anybody who is stepping out of their comfort zone does.

So I'm stood tall, looking out to the audience before me (in my mind I'm on stage) when Josie says "Jessica, breathe." I look at her. "What do you mean, breathe?" She said "You look petrified!"

Josie was right, I wasn't breathing to feel comfortable in my tall posture. I was holding my tall posture to show off. And it was stiff. And it looked uncomfortable. And I was embarrassed. There I was, a person claiming to be 'fit' with an athletic dance background, and an ability to work my body, and yet I had absolutely no understanding of how to work *with* my own body. And suddenly it all made sense...

Over a period of almost two years, I had developed 'stage fright', where I'd become terrified to perform. It had started with not trusting my movement memory, and then it quickly developed into being sick due to terrible stomach pains. I'd lost my appetite when approaching performance tours and I was becoming miserable with anxiety. That's when I decided to pack up my leg warmers.

Nicole, my Pilates teacher trainer told me to practise my comfortable tall posture at any opportunity - in a queue at the shop, when sat in class, when making my evening dinner... "At any opportunity".

And that's exactly what I did do. I began lengthening through my spine, taking deep breaths in and slowly exhaling and opening the base of my skull when I was walking down stairs, when I was sat at my computer, when I was walking to the corner shop. Not only was I looking relaxed, I was feeling happier too. Oh yes, I also took the lift at any opportunity I could rather than walking upstairs because I could then check my posture out in the mirror, haha... basically I became a little bit obsessed with breathing while lengthening my posture.

And then I figured I was going over the top. I didn't need to practise all.the.time!

So as I was making a delicious cup of Yorkshire Tea, I realised that was the perfect opportunity - to breathe, pull up tall through the crown of my head, draw my shoulders back and tilt my pelvis to engage my light beams while making a cuppa.

And so I pass this little secret daily reminder onto you: experience your head to tailbone posture when making a cuppa. And keep your notebook close, because you will start to notice an awareness of sensations pretty much instantly,

Energise The Base Of Your Skull

Yin and Yang With Earth

The focus of 'Alignment Of The Serpent' is to show you how to engage your powerful posture erector spinae muscles. By strengthening your back to hold your spine and ribs upright against the pull of gravity, you are protecting your spleen and stomach.

During this section in the Feel Alive Program, I'm often asked "How does gravity affect my spleen and stomach?"

To answer that question, I have to go back to basics with you...

Qi is life force holding the body strong against the pull of gravity. It travels to all organ meridians around the body as movement, action and energy. The spleen stores qi which is released during the digestion process.

There are five functions of your digestive system:

Ingestion: Food is taken in to your body via your mouth. It takes approximately 20 minutes for food to arrive into your stomach.

Digestion: Solid food is broken down into smaller pieces by the churning of your stomach and the chemical break down of large molecules in your stomach, and small intestine. Food stays in your stomach for approximately five hours.

Absorption: A network of blood and lymph vessels transport nutrients to various parts of your body in your small intestine. It is at this stage when clean qi is sent to your spleen.

Assimilation: Vitamins and minerals travel across to the blood capillaries of your small intestine to assist in cell metabolism and the healthy functioning of your body. This is your post-natal jing in action.

Elimination & Defecation: Dirty qi and waste is transported to your large intestine to be stored before leaving your body via your anal canal.

In Traditional Chinese Medicine, the yin spleen is paired with the yang stomach, and they both not only digest food but they are also stimulated by absorbing information (from television, computers, smart phones etc.) through the body's nervous system and its senses.

You know how we, as a population, are often told to switch off electronics before bed? Well, in TCM, the spleen is related to thoughts, and the stimulus our senses get from looking at electronic devices goes straight to the spleen for processing before the nervous system transports the information up to the brain. Imagine the overload of information going on in the yin spleen before bed... yikes, no wonder we're always tired!

When overloaded, the parasympathetic nervous system, which runs inside your spinal column, increases gastro-intestinal tract activity and overstimulates digestion processes; creating tension in your stomach, such as indigestion and solid waste problems. The yang essence is now weak and the yin action is in excess. You know what I'm going to say don't you... disharmony.

When the stomach and spleen are in disharmony, the earth element is affected. The earth element represents having solid roots - being grounded with clarity of thought and restful emotions.

Let's take another look at the complex Wu Xing cycle. The diagram can be found in 'The Wu Xing' chapter.

When your body is in balance, your stomach and spleen (earth) are generated by your small intestine and heart (fire), which are generated by your gallbladder and liver (wood). Your gallbladder and liver are nourished by your urinary bladder and kidneys (water) which are cared for by your large intestine and lungs (metal). Your large intestine and lungs are generated by your stomach and spleen. The harmony goes full circle.

Now, when your earth element in your digestive system is lacking nourishment it attacks the urinary system: your water element, which attacks the cardiovascular system, your fire element. Your cardiovascular system then attacks the respiratory system: your metal element. Your respiratory system then attacks the nervous system, your wood element, which then attacks the digestive system.

In response to this organic chaos, your body becomes sensitive; your mouth starts to feel sore, your muscles ache and your touch becomes more attuned to sensations, particularly your thumb. Have you ever been so incredibly stressed that your thumb goes numb? It's really odd because it's not pins and needles numb and it's not blocked circulation (like when you fall asleep on your arm) numb; it's more like a cold numb.

This is the effect of gravity on your spleen and stomach. I must make a point here that if you do experience a numb sensation often, please have a quick chat with your doctor about it, if you haven't already.

In a nutshell, as I mentioned before, qi is stored in your spleen. Qi circulates your body as a clear fluid just under the surface of your skin. Its role is to transport yang energy to all parts of your body with an overall job of holding your body upright against the pull of gravity. Over stimulation, worry and stress, basically thinking deeply for a long period of time, cause disharmony within your spleen, which is a yin organ.

Its paired yang organ, the stomach, digests and metabolises nutrients from the earth's offerings into yin jing energy.

When you are stressing out, over thinking and worrying, your yang qi flow is restricted which gives rise to an excess of yin within your body. And as you now know, when yin and yang are not balanced, the body reacts. In this situation, qi cannot provide enough life force to hold the body up against the pull of gravity, and as a result the body's posture changes. Guess where the major shift is... you've got it, at the occipital.

The nerves supply from your brain branch out at the occipital area to your hands. With poor posture at the occipital, and compression in the neck vertebrae, the nerves often get pinched resulting in the nervous system delaying signals to your hands. This creates pins & needles and numbness. Because gravity pulls organs down, the spleen and stomach have now become compressed, and their efficiency to release qi energy is compromised. We're in the circle of disharmony!

Feeling odd sensations in the thumb is a sign of stress within the digestive system. During my transition to relaxed health, it became clear that my 'dead thumb' should not be ignored.

By understanding that the body needs additional support to counteract the pull of gravity, we can clearly see that the erector spinae muscles have to be strong and cared for in order for the body to understand that support is required.

'Alignment Of The Serpent' corrects your cervical spine and sacrum posture, assisting your stomach and spleen to connect with the earth element to ease worry and stress within the digestive system.

So how did I relax my anxiety and ease my stomach problems? I started practising morning 'Pillow Pilates' movements.

Execute Pulling Tall Through The Crown Of Your Head

'Pillow Pilates' Cervical Spine Morning Movement

Pilates was my antidote to becoming overwhelmed with stress and allowing (subconsciously) my body to adapt and change in a detrimental way.

Alongside my daily practise of pulling tall through the crown of my head, I performed a quick and effective morning movement to increase strength and rotation of my spine with exaggerated lengthening through my erector spinae from head to tail.

Here I've written the instructions to 'Spine Twist' in clear and concise stages for you to follow. Simple reminder instructions for you to copy, if you feel following these instructions are too detailed, are at the back of this book in the 'What Next?' chapter. These instructions are here for you to fully understand the movements and breath work involved.

As you perform these actions on top of your mattress, make sure to engage your lumbar powerful posture and your thoracic powerful posture - remember to shine your beams ;-) And pull up tall through the crown of your head.

Spine Twist is one of my favourite movements of the 'Pillow Pilates' syllabus because it not only strengthens the spine muscles, it opens the chest and works the leg muscles too!

Start by sitting upright as tall as you can, just as a toddler does, on top of your mattress with your legs stretched out in front of you and your arms stretching forward at shoulder height. Your elbows should be soft with your palms facing down. Your legs should be hip distance apart and your shoulders should be down in your back. Relax your feet. Inhale deeply. Exhale to lengthen your spine through the crown of your head and engage your latissimus dorsi muscle.

Breathe in to pull your right elbow behind you, while stretching your left fingers toward your left foot. Inhale again to twist your waist, turning your head to look over your right shoulder. Keep your right elbow lifted to ensure your armpit is hollowed. Think of gently twisting your ribcage on the first pulse and your spine on the second. Keep super tall through your beautiful shiny pearls in your spine!

Exhale to return to the starting position with your arms mirroring your legs, sitting tall with your pelvis beams shining forward.

Inhale to pulse your left elbow twice, leading with your bent elbow first and then a second time turning your head to look over your left shoulder.

Exhale to return to the starting position with your arms mirroring your legs, again sitting tall with your pelvis beams shining forward.

Repeat five times each side, alternating sides. So you will gently twist to look over your right shoulder, return to centre, gently twist to look over your left shoulder, return to centre, gently twist to look over your right shoulder, return to centre, gently twist to look over your left shoulder etc...

ATTENTION: It is important to twist on the in-breath so you are supporting your lungs and diaphragm in assisting your erector spinae to control your movement.

After your fifth gentle twist to look over your left shoulder, return to centre on your exhale. Inhale to pull taller through the crown of your head, and as you exhale, gently relax your spine and hug both your knees into your chest. Take a few deep breaths to relax.

Make sure to write your journal notes as you experience new body connections. Your future self will absolutely love reading your journal!

After a few months of looking after myself, I read through my journal. Wow! Be prepared for some pretty amazing stuff! I almost cried when I read through my notes a few months after my 'epiphany' moment with Josie because I realised I had connected to my body - I now understand how to positively respond to my stomach when it gives me signs that it is not understanding me.

'Alignment Of The Serpent' works your erector spinae muscles; strengthening your back, correcting poor neck posture which effectively opens the meridian channels to your digestive system, which then eases your stomach and spleen jing energy, boosting the flow of earth element to stimulate your body confidence.

I now announce on my Feel Alive Program "If you don't understand your body; Your body doesn't understand you."

Co-ordination Of The Horse

Embrace Your Yin and Yang With Confidence

Connecting your lungs and large intestine

with your intercostal muscles and respiratory system

to the element metal for alignment

of your dynamic emotions.

"What are we going to do without?"

Ooh please!

"What are we going to do without?"

Let me breathe!

"What are we going to do without?"

Ooh, quick!

"We are all going to die without!

Breathe in deep!"

- Kate Bush 'Breathing' lyrics

Did you know we take approximately 25,000 breaths every day? Without affecting our spleen or our nervous system by stressing or worrying about it, we just do it without thinking. That alone is why I'm so goose bumpy about the human body... We are magicians and we don't even know it!

I used to know a magician. Not as in the hocus pocus magic. And not as in the children's birthday parties card trick magic. He was magic with his hands. He played the piano beautifully. Each time I visited him in his studio, he would play a silly ditty which instantly got me laughing and wiggling my bottom. Haha, oh we laughed!

James, when I knew him, was a 56 year old touring musician. He travelled the globe playing keyboards for session bands, travelling by aeroplane often and staying in hotels regularly. And he lived the stereotype rock and roll lifestyle of booze, smokes, and late nights.

Exciting hey? Well, not for James. He was tired of visiting a new city three times a week, and he was tired of not feeling quite himself.

I knew James personally, so I could see the change in him each time we met for catch up coffee. On one particular coffchat date, I had to ask him "James, are you looking after yourself?"

He then looked at me with dispassion "Jessica, darling, how is it possible to look after myself with my job? I work crazy hours, I don't rest, my body is already knackered with this cold I've had for weeks, again! And to top it off I'm developing a 'rotund' belly. I mean... what's that all about!?"

My reply "James, you need me in your life. We'll co-ordinate your horse".

'Co-ordination Of The Horse' looks into the connection between the way your emotions affect the way you hold yourself and the support your posture provides to your lungs. Correct breathing is massively important to your physiological and psychological wellbeing.

Engage Your Ribs

Principle of Belly Button into Spine Posture

Accurate posture plays a huge role in correct breathing, and it is so simple to achieve when you know how to engage your internal intercostal muscles with your diaphragm and belly button.

When you inhale, your lungs grow bigger, your ribs expand as they move away from your spine, your spine curves increase, your shoulders roll forward and your diaphragm drops. As you exhale, your lungs reduce in size, your spine curves shorten, your ribs narrow, your shoulders slide down your back and your diaphragm lifts.

Over the years, as your body develops habits which make movement easier and quicker; your muscles relax and your body posture and breathing movements reduce; resulting in a heavy looking physique, such as a rotund belly, and laboured body actions.

Your internal and external intercostal muscles are major muscles within your chest wall, positioned between each of your ribs.

Your external intercostal muscles are the outer layer of muscles which work in co-ordination with your diaphragm to aid your in-breath. Your internal intercostal muscles are responsible for breath control and some upper body movements. They also co-ordinate to support your body's centre of gravity. When you understand how to control your ribs to support your body, your whole posture completely changes. It is like magic.

'Suck your belly button into your spine' is the 'Feel Alive System' principle of 'Co-ordination Of The Horse'. It is a metaphor to close your ribs by consciously engaging your internal intercostal muscles and pulling your waist in.

In 'Endurance Of The Fish', 'Breath Of The Bird', and 'Alignment Of The Serpent' you learnt about your spine posture. You should engage those three principles in addition to 'Co-ordination Of The Horse'.

So I'm going to jump straight in and invite you to do an exercise now, which is what I asked James to do while he was sat at his piano.

Stand or sit tall - pull tall through the crown of your head and tilt your chin in slightly to open the base of your skull. Draw your shoulders back so your upper region spine is long, and your shoulder blades are flat in your back with your latissimus dorsi muscle engaged. Tilt your pelvis forward slightly so you are long through your tailbone and open through the vertebrae of your lower spine, let your beams shine ;-)

Place a hand on your upper abdomen (the gap at the front of your ribs). Now, take a deep breath in. Fill your lungs. Stretch your external intercostal muscles and let your belly relax.

Slowly empty your lungs. Breathe out through your mouth. As you do that, pull tall through your spine (head to tailbone) and feel your internal intercostal muscles close your ribs tighter, so they feel to be getting smaller in width. Exhale more to the very last drop of air and suck your belly button into your spine.

Do you feel the muscles in your abdomen strengthen and the sides of your rib cage and back narrow?

Keep those muscles working and take another deep inhale through your nose. This time consciously feel the breath laterally, so you are keeping your belly button sucked in and the gap between your ribs closed; your breath is filling the sides of your ribs without moving your belly area.

The analogy I use when explaining this exercise is, I know, primary school level but it does make sense...

Imagine you are in an electric toaster and you need to keep your ribs closed and belly pulled in, in order to not get burnt!

ATTENTION: Remember to keep long and open in the base of your skull. Do not let your shoulders lift up to your ears as you inhale. Keep your latissimus dorsi muscle engaged to keep your chest proud. And remember to breathe fully.

How super strong and tall do you feel right now? Do you feel like a warrior ready to take on the world? That's the analogy James came up with, and I borrowed it from him :-)

So here is your journal task. I want you to 'Create Your Confidence' by taking on the characteristics of a super strong person - someone who impresses you.

Someone who looks strong and moves with balanced energy, with bravery and composure. Adopt the posture that person holds. I don't mean for you to act out the actions. I do mean I want you to imagine their posture and adapt your posture to mirror theirs. Write a short statement about how you feel as that person, and say how easy, or not, it is to hold the posture.

I think of myself as Kate Bush with energy from her flexible waist effortlessly filling every inch of her body to allow her to fly through her dance routines.

It is really beneficial for us to keep a record of how we feel in this beginning stage of practising powerful posture so we can recognise later how amazingly dynamic our bodies are as we develop.

Just as we unconsciously breathe 25,000 times per day; it takes 10,000 repetitions of consciously practising something for it to be in our movement memory and become unconscious habit. So you should practise your *'pull tall through the crown of your head'*, *'draw your shoulders back'*, *'tilt your pelvis in-line'* and *'suck your belly button into your spine'* powerful posture, when possible, every day.

Experience Your Ribs

A Daily Reminder to Empty Your Lungs

We learn in high school that our two lungs are cone shaped spongy organs that sit inside our rib cage on either side of our heart and above our diaphragm. We also learn that respiration is the process of gas exchange and the use of air within our body. If you asked someone "Why do we breathe?" they would possibly say "Breathing ensures that all your body's cells receive oxygen and gets rid of carbon dioxide so all your body systems function efficiently".

Great. But what if you asked that person "How often do you consciously breathe?" You probably wouldn't get a proper answer.

Have a go at fully filling your lungs now. Take a deep breath in through your nose to fully expand your external intercostal muscles. Breathe in to your lungs maximum potential and then slowly let the breath go with a "huhhhhh". It actually feels, surprising, great doesn't it? So why do we take this essential life giving action for granted?

The answer is beyond my comprehension, but I can take something from the question... I can understand that I should practise conscious breathing regularly.

We all suffer from a little bit of self-conscious modesty. We all feel silly and 'showy offy' (to quote my dad) when we stand taller than our comfort allows us. But where does a lack of confidence come from - why? Remember in my introduction I tell you about ancient Tao folk connecting to their dragon, and that the dragon became a symbol of power for those who are worthy? Well, aren't you worthy of feeling powerful? I say yes!

So forget your comfort zone. Forget feeling silly. Start experiencing the principle of *'sucking your belly button into your spine'* every day.

Practise it on any walk you take, it could be walking to your car or taking a hike up Mount Emei. Wherever you are, suck your belly button in to lift your waist and connect your ribs with your breath.

Honestly, it is amazing how powerful your walk becomes with this principle.

As you walk, make sure to *engage your latissimus dorsi muscle, tilt your pelvis in-line* and *pull up tall through the crown of your head* while you empty your lungs to close your ribs - *suck your belly button in to your spine.*

It really is important to connect all four principles together at this stage of owning a powerful posture, because if you're not careful your spine will push down into a deeper unbalanced curve and your shoulders will lift up into a top region breath, which is not natural or beneficial for your vibrant health. So walk tall, walk strong, walk with confidence! Remember to write notes in your notebook related to your experience with your powerful posture.

Similarly, keep in mind that strutting like a top model down your local high street could look a bit odd. Stay natural with a strong gait. Think more Bruce Springsteen and less Mick Jagger.

Talking of rock stars, James totally loved this exercise. Even during our first session in his music studio; where he stood up, exaggerated his 'rotund' belly and gurned at me, he quickly got serious and seriously embraced his tall posture.

"Everything feels to click into place. I feel lighter, the waistband on my pants feels slacker and I feel almost as though a gentle force is guiding me forward when I walk. I'm not sluggish in my movement, which is an unusual feeling. OK, in my imagination I feel like David Beckham. Haha." - James's journal entry.

Energise Your Breath

Yin and Yang With Metal

Breath is vital to life. True. Strong posture improves our breathing. Correct. Is that all? No.

The respiratory system is a wonderful thing. It serves many important functions for creating happiness in everyday living.

We often hear how detoxing the body is necessary for improving positive emotions. Did you know there are three methods of detoxing the body to feel alive and full of vibrant health? In all three ways, correct breathing is the foundation.

Carbon dioxide is a natural gas that can be toxic to the body. It is a by-product of metabolised carbon in food and water reacting with inhaled oxygen. Strong healthy breath detoxes the body of carbon dioxide by exhaling air from the lungs. Strong healthy breath is regarded as an equal balance of inhale and exhale.

Toxins are also removed from the body as sweat on your skin. In TCM, skin is considered to be the third lung. The pores of the skin are seen as the 'doors of qi', allowing energy to flow into and out of the body. When the skin looks weak, it is said that the lungs need the flow of clean breath [equal full breaths].

Your large intestine is the yang to your yin lungs. Along with the breath from your lungs and sweat from your skin, the large intestine plays a massive role in eliminating toxins from the body as solid toxic waste.

Oxygen in the blood stream assists the body in absorbing all the nutrients and water it needs. The nutrients are transported as post-natal jing to the kidneys and helps to create mucus which moves the solid toxic waste (poo) out of the body.

Traditional Chinese Medicine looks on breathing as giving the body life; it is the activity of air in the lungs that drives qi around the body and nourishes the large intestine for post-natal jing movement of waste elimination. Remember that yang qi and yin jing must be in balance for the body to be in vibrant health.

If you do not breathe correctly, the oxygen levels in the blood are reduced and qi cannot flow adequately to remove the waste easily from the body. In TCM this is known as yang deficiency.

It only takes a day to start feeling the effects of yang deficiency, resulting in toxic build up. Common symptoms include constipation, frequent colds, aggravated asthma, headaches, skin psoriasis and negative emotions.

These symptoms are lousy and they make us feel lousy, and totally not our-self. They make us feel bloated and heavy, and unable to concentrate. They make us feel stressed.

Stress is commonly regarded as physical or emotional strain and it usually creates muscle tension. This muscle tension is common around the upper body region - shoulders, neck, head and even the arms and fingers. Isn't it just so easy to 'sink' when you're feeling rubbish; to let your upper body drop into your lower region, to let your belly hang out and to let your head drop forward? That is qi deficiency at its best right there!

So what could be causing James to be feeling 'not quite himself'?

We can look at the Traditional Chinese Medicine theory of Wu Xing, the diagram is in 'The Wu Xing' chapter if you haven't copied it into your notebook, linking his lungs and large intestine with the element metal, to get an idea. As you are now aware from learning about wood, fire and earth; everything is connected.

When your body is in balance, your lungs and large intestine (metal) are generated by your spleen and stomach (earth), which are generated by your heart and small intestine (fire). They are nourished by your liver and gallbladder (wood) which are cared for by your kidneys and urinary bladder (water). These are generated by your lungs and large intestine. The harmony goes full circle.

If your lungs or large intestine (metal) are lacking nourishment they attack the nervous system: your liver and gallbladder (wood). Your wood element is now in disharmony with the digestive system: your spleen and stomach (earth) which attacks the urinary system: your kidneys and urinary bladder (water). Your water element then attacks the cardiovascular system: your heart and small intestine (fire), which then attack the respiratory system.   Your body is in total disharmony.

Because metal is a malleable element, in TCM it is associated with the ebb and flow of life and the changes we experience. The metal element is associated with intuition and rationality. Usually when a person is suffering disharmony in the lungs and large intestine, their emotions are affected: they find they are unable to let go of past experiences and perhaps thoughts of what might have been. These feelings are often regarded as grief; grieving the past.

By co-ordinating the flow of qi energy with the inhale of oxygen and the essence of jing for waste elimination, the metal element can be at ease and the body can efficiently detox.

James was living, in standard comparison, a bonkers lifestyle. He was regularly smoking tobacco and drinking alcohol in excess. He wasn't resting often and his body was tired; his posture was reflecting unhappiness and his emotions were up and down "one minute I'm loving life, the next I find myself crying, hating my job and wishing I had a different life".

According to James, he was showing signs of exhaustion and could do with a few days bed rest. The TCM theory looks from another perspective.

Let's take a look at the Wu Xing diagram again to understand what's going on. DO NOT worry if you don't understand the Wu Xing cycle; as I said in 'Endurance Of The Fish', it takes months for students at Traditional Chinese Medical School to learn and fully understand the concept.

James' liver and gallbladder were working hard because of excessive consumption of alcohol and cigarettes. This created a weakness in the functioning of his yin liver, and affected the qi flowing smoothly to other meridians in his body. Because his yin jing energy was working harder to process the toxic substances in his liver, there was an excess of yang from his gallbladder in his wood element.

The imbalance meant wood was not nourishing his fire element in the generating cycle. His heart and small intestine started to give him a warning by showing emotional signs of passion ("loving life") and hate ("hating my job"). The disturbance in his yin and yang balance meant his fire element was attacking his lungs. He experienced this by regularly suffering with a mucus cold, feeling sad emotions and generally not feeling himself.

But unfortunately, James' lungs were already weak because his heavy posture was reducing the amount of oxygen he could breathe in. So his water element was already not getting as much nourishment as it should.

Looking at the Wu Xing diagram, can you guess what yin and yang element James needed to boost to bring his body back to life? If you think it is water, then you are correct. Virtual high five to you.

Remember in 'Endurance Of The Fish' we learnt that the liver is a massive organ and it is incredibly enduring - it can work super hard for a long time under intense conditions. Taking into consideration James' symptoms, we can assume that the liver is not the root of James' problems.

In order to boost an element, its 'mother' element needs a little bit more energy. The water element's mother is metal - the lungs and large intestine! Now we're really getting into how things are connected.

James needed to remedy the root of his health problem, and that was going to be by breathing correctly. Oxygen in the blood stream assists in the transportation of post-natal jing to the kidneys (water element).

Can you relate to James' situation? I know I can. And I know that when I've had a hectic schedule where I've started to feel rundown, easily upset and feeling snotty with mucus; I've boosted my metal energy by performing the 'Pillow Pilates Co-ordination Of The Horse Morning Movement Routine'.

The deep, controlled breathing along with exercises that strengthen the intercostal muscles increase oxygen levels within the blood, stimulate the yin and yang organs, and relax muscular tension.

By performing Co-ordination Of The Horse 'Single Leg Stretch', you are engaging the intercostal muscles and the diaphragm. Even if you don't experience any of the symptoms of a weak metal element, it is still a really great exercise to do for your breath control. In addition, your body will balance emotions, gain mental clarity and boost your body functions, all before you've got out of bed :-)

Execute Sucking Your Belly Into Spine

'Pillow Pilates' Breath Control Morning Movement

Here I've written the instructions to 'Single Leg Stretch' in clear and concise stages for you to follow. Simple reminder instructions for you to copy if you feel following these instructions are too detailed are at the back of this book in the 'What Next?' chapter. These instructions are here for you to fully understand the movements and breath work involved.

Before you begin, make sure to engage the four principles you now know: *pull tall through the crown of your head, draw your shoulders back, tilt your pelvis in-line* and *suck your belly button into your spine.*

Lay on your back on top of your mattress with the covers pulled back; you will need space to move your legs. Rest your arms at your sides, and bend your knees so your feet are flat on the mattress. Make sure your feet are hip distance apart - you need your pelvis to be aligned and you should feel long through your tailbone. Breathe in through your nose to fill your lungs.

As you breathe out lift your right foot off the mattress to bring your right knee, in a 90 degree angle, over your right hip. Keep your left knee bent with your left foot on the mattress. Empty your lungs to the very last drop of air to engage your internal intercostal muscles.

Keep your ribs closed and your shoulders down away from your ears as you inhale. Exhale to stretch your right leg away from your pelvis.

Keep your toes in-line with your right hip - DO NOT let your leg move out wide to the side. Stretch your leg to be parallel to your left thigh. Don't go too low just yet.

Breathe in to bring your right leg back to a 90 degree bend at your knee, over your right hip.

Breathe out to stretch your right leg away again. Make sure to stretch long through the back of your knee.

Breathe in to bring your right knee back to a 90 degree bend over your right hip again.

Breathe out, using your internal intercostal muscles to close your ribs if they have opened slightly. Stretch your right leg away, feeling long through the back of your knee. This time lower your leg a little more to open and stretch your psoas muscle in your right hip.

Breathe in to bend your right knee over your right hip.

Repeat the stretch another 8 times, so you are doing the 'Single Right Leg Stretch' a total of 10 times.

To finish, breathe in to bend your right knee over your right hip and breathe out to lower your right foot down to the mattress, keeping your right knee bent. Make sure to keep the length through your tailbone so you are not arching your lower back.

Repeat the action, this time with your left leg stretching away from your pelvis.

Breathe in through your nose to fill your lungs. As you breathe out lift your left foot off the mattress to bring your left knee, in a 90 degree angle, over your left hip. Keep your right knee bent with your right foot on the mattress, and both arms stretching at your sides, palms resting on the mattress. Empty your lungs to the very last drop of air to engage your internal intercostal muscles as you stretch your left leg away.

Repeat your 'Single Left Leg Stretch' 10 times.

ATTENTION: On each exhale empty your lungs, engage your intercostal muscles and suck your belly button into your spine. Keep your ears away from your shoulders and keep long through your tailbone – don't allow your lower back to arch.

To finish, gently drop both your legs down onto the mattress. Take a deep inhale to stretch long through both legs, pulling tall through the crown of your head and lengthening your tailbone away. Breathe out to relax. Take a few moments to bring your breathing back to normal.

WARNING: You might feel a little bit light headed at first when you are taking your deep breaths. This is good because it is a sign your qi is moving around your body. You may also experience a light headache after your first few days of practising this deep breathing. Don't be put off by the effects of deep breathing. This is also good because it is a sign that your body is eliminating toxins. Make sure to drink plenty of room temperature water after your 'Single Leg Stretch' movement and the headaches should pass pretty quickly.

'Co-ordination Of The Horse' works your intercostal muscles; strengthens your ribs, and corrects your breathing which opens the meridians to your respiratory system, stimulates your lungs and large intestine, boosts your body's detox process and the flow of qi around your body, creating dynamic, vibrant and happy energy.

Control Of The Ox

Embrace Your Yin and Yang For Life Balanced Shen

Connecting your kidneys and urinary bladder

with your pelvic floor muscle and urinary system

to the water element for a dazzling vibrant shine.

"I fear not the man who has practised 10,000 kicks once;

I fear the man who has practised one kick 10,000 times."

- Bruce Lee

The final story within this compendium is slightly different from the previous ones. 'Control Of The Ox' tells of a man who feels positive connections within his body in many ways. It's the perfect story, really, to conclude our journey to powerful posture.

This story illustrates to you the power you have within you. Generally, people in the west are not educated to understand and connect with the power within them. I appreciate that sounds sci fi and whacky, but it is a fundamental truth.

In the east, there's all sorts of documented accounts of the power of qi; particularly surrounding martial arts where practitioners understand how to harness their yin and yang energies. It is believed that anybody can learn this. We are all given the yin - yang polarity on conception, but it takes discipline and awareness of your connections to awaken and control it.

It is common practise in western medicine to fix our poorly working body quick with over the counter medication. And if that medication doesn't work, we try a prescribed medicine.

The east practise energy work. It is believed that our body is an electric magnetic field which is affected by our thoughts, feelings, activities, the food we eat, our lifestyle and the natural energy that surrounds us and also, in our modern world, the unnatural energy such as smart phones, computers, televisions etc.

Acupuncture, Reflexology, Full Body Massage, and Martial Arts (Qi Gong, Kung Fu, Tai Chi) are practised daily to balance and regulate the body and the mind, generating a long and healthy life. Herbal medicine is the root of Chinese Medicine, taken as the alternative to prescribed drugs.

In this final story, I'm going to share with you my experience with Mr Liu. He is my calligraphy teacher. He is also a martial arts expert, having practised Kung Fu for over two decades.

I'd love to say the reason I go to calligraphy class is because I'm awesome at writing Chinese characters, but in truth I'm terrible. I go for the laughter and the silliness we all share. Often Mr Liu will start teasing one of us students and suddenly the room is full of "huanliu, huanliu, dayingzhang. Hahahaha."

It was during one of these spontaneous Kung Fu fights that I realised my theory on body connections being vital to vibrant health is actually not so far removed from the Eastern perspective, as I had naively thought!

Mr Liu was demonstrating to me a deep seated position of the pelvis in relation to a wide base position of the feet. From this position, one can sway, twist, breathe and attack with solid foundation. We were practising together when I noticed Mr Liu was asking me to copy his hand movements. He cupped his left hand over his right and placed them palms face up just under his stomach. "Power" he said.

Hash tag mouth drop to the floor. Did Mr Liu just tell me his power comes from his pelvic floor muscle? I looked at him "Shenme?" ("Pardon").

"Here" He stood behind me, wrapped his arms around my waist, took hold of both my hands and placed them on my lower pelvis, where my pelvic floor muscle is located.

As geeky as it might seem to you, this was another epiphany moment for me!

Engage Your Lower Dantian

Principle of Squeeze Your Pelvic Floor Muscle

It is a common misconception that only women have a pelvic floor muscle. Indeed men do have one too, and when trained it can be very effective in the bedroom, wink wink.

The pelvic floor muscle acts as a harness between your anus and your pubic bone. Although it is hidden from view, your pelvic floor muscle can be, and should be, controlled consciously. When you strengthen your pelvic floor muscle, you are awakening the meridian to your kidneys, which invigorates your jing essence. You are also lifting and distributing the weight of your urinary bladder and bowels, which creates a stronger pelvis area and a flattened and lighter waistline. Try it...

Imagine you really need a wee. Suck the internal pelvis area in and up, as you do when needing the toilet. When I'm teaching 1:1, I get a little personal and tell men to move their penis, without their hands, and I tell women to suck their vagina closed. It is graphic, but it gets the pelvic floor muscle engaged!

That is the action of engaging the front of the pelvic floor muscle; you now need to engage the back. Do this by squeezing your bum. I don't mean forcefully squeeze your bum cheeks, I mean suck your anus up. It is the sensation you get when you are desperate to poo and someone else is in the toilet room. Engage all four other principles: *pull tall through the crown of your head, draw your shoulders back, tilt your pelvis in-line* and *suck your belly button into your spine.* You are now squeezing the front and back of your pelvic floor muscle. Can you feel it? Make sure to suck in and pull up, rather than push – you don't want to wee yourself!

In Traditional Chinese Medicine, the pelvic floor muscle is known as the 'internal power' and it is exercised, nourished, and appreciated as the generator of yin and yang. It is the place in the abdominal field where we supply the body with stored qi from the spleen, and life essence pre-natal jing from the kidneys. It is the place where Qi Gong experts focus their mind seconds before doing extraordinary things. Mr Liu showed me photographs of his friend; a man so intuitively connected to his qi and body functions that he had broken a pile of three stone tablets, with his bare hand!

Other incredible energy transference stories from Mr Liu include a man named Zhou Ting-Jue. Master Zhou is a Tai Chi and Kung Fu Grand Master in China. Mr Liu's eyes were on fire with excitement as he expressed to me he had "met and watched him set fire to a newspaper." Okay, so maybe I should've been more excited in my communication with Mr Liu, but I didn't get why that was so thrilling. "Power of qi (huge smiling face)". Oh... Ohhhhhh, I got it. Oh wow, Master Zhou connected to his lower dantian, generated qi energy through his body to his hand and presented it by setting fire to newspaper!

In Eastern philosophy, the body is divided into three energy centre's; the dantians. The lower dantian is below your belly button, close to your pubic bone. The middle is within your thoracic cavity, just behind your heart. The upper is at the front of your brain. When the three are nurtured, the body (jing), mind (qi) and spirit (shen) glow with radiance and health.

All martial arts students begin their body-mind training by focusing on the lower dantian. So why not make 'Ride The Wave' our first exercise of Control Of The Ox...

Have your notebook close by. Before we begin, I'd like you to write, or draw if you prefer, a description of how you feel right now. Forget about your superficial emotions, like "I've just had to clean the coffee cup ring again from the kitchen worktop, why can't people clean up after themselves." These emotions are ego feelings and they soon pass. I want you to focus on your deep emotions. Where are you feeling you hold your energy? For example, do you suffer with ear problems such as tinnitus? Are you usually smart and witty, but recently you've noticed you're more often absentminded? Do you fear 'what if' situations now more than you used to? Anything you feel is impacting your everyday life, write it down.

Take another deep breath in through your nose to fill your lungs, counting to five. Breathe out to completely empty your lungs, counting to five. Start by sitting comfortably. Engage the four powerful posture principles: *pull tall through the crown of your head, draw your shoulders back, tilt your pelvis in-line* and *suck your belly button into your spine*, and take a deep breath in.

As you inhale, lift your front pelvic floor muscle. Imagine you have an elevator inside your lower abdominal region with five levels. Lift your front pelvic floor muscle to level one. Breathe out to gently release the lift. Repeat the breath, this time lifting to level two. Gently release the lift on your exhale. Continue breathing in through your nose and out through your mouth to work through each level. DO NOT push your release, otherwise you will wee!

At level five, hold the front pelvic floor muscle lift whilst you exhale. This time on your inhale squeeze your bottom (anus) to match the sucking up of your front pelvic floor muscle.

We're now going to 'Ride The Wave'. This can be quite challenging, but keep going because you will have your lightbulb moment.

Exhale a long breath and gently release your anus squeeze. On the same exhale after your anus release, gently release your front pelvic floor muscle. Inhale a long breath to squeeze your bottom (anus) to level five, followed by lifting your front pelvic floor muscle to level five. Exhale to gently release your anus squeeze followed by a gentle release of your front pelvic floor muscle.

Repeat this wave action no more than five times, because over stimulating the qi in your lower dantian can have the opposite effect on creating energy, so make sure you're aware of how many repetitions you are completing.

After your fifth wave, gently lift both your front pelvic floor muscle and your anus to level three. Relax your breathing to a normal rhythm and take a moment to connect to your emotions.

How do you feel? Most people experience a light fluttering in the base of their pelvis, almost like an electric current. This is great, this is your qi working. If you don't experience this fluttering sensation immediately, don't be disappointed... keep practising 'Ride The Wave' daily because it will come.

Write in your notebook any feelings or thoughts you experience. Write the date and a short title, so you can recall the experience when you look over your journal in the future.

'Suck your pelvic floor muscle and squeeze your bum' is one of the 'Feel Alive System' principles to powerful posture, and it is the martial arts principle of lower dantian engagement.

Experience Your Lower Dantian

A Daily Reminder to Squeeze Your Bum

As I mentioned in 'Co-ordination Of The Horse', anything you do should be practised 10,000 times for it to become habit. We can learn from Bruce Lee, a world famous martial arts icon, that theory is also the same when training your body. In my Feel Alive Program, I say it takes 20,000 correct repetitions of an action for it to be mastered and in your lifelong muscle memory.

However, you are clearly not going to be a Kung Fu Master by sucking your pelvic floor muscle and squeezing your bum 20,000 times. This incredible feat takes decades of meditation and Qi Gong exercise to expertise. Over time, though, you are connecting to your lower dantian, engaging your kidney and urinary bladder support and strengthening your urinary system.

The lower dantian is closely connected to pre and post-natal jing essence. When our jing is strong and our lower dantian is engaged, we are dazzling, active and glowing with health. All emotions are balanced and our mind is alert and open.

You learnt in 'Breath Of The Bird' pre-natal jing is stored in the kidneys and post-natal jing is formed in the kidneys, which are your two yin organs to your yang urinary bladder organ.

Your kidneys are bean shaped yin organs in the back of your abdomen, one on either side of your spine. Because your liver is larger on your right side, your right kidney is slightly lower than your left kidney.

Your yin kidneys filter waste from your blood and reabsorb non-toxic materials back into your blood stream. They regulate water and salt balance, form urine and regulate blood pressure and blood volume. The filtration process in your kidneys regulates the PH in your body's fluid and maintains the water and electrolyte balance in your body (jing).

Your ureters transports urine from your kidneys to your urinary bladder, where it is stored. Your urinary bladder is a pear shaped yang organ located just above your pubic bone. A strong urinary bladder allows us to be active without weeing ourselves. These organs function together as the urinary system and we should support them by strengthening our pelvic floor muscle.

A fabulous daily reminder to strengthen your pelvic floor muscle is: 'see a red traffic light: suck your pelvic floor muscle and squeeze your bum'.

I love this daily reminder because it reminds me of the early noughties (the year 2001 ish), when people would say "I'm lifting my pelvic floor and you don't even know it" with a smirk and a little naughty twinkle in their eye. Well, that's exactly what I think when I'm driving my car and stop at a red light. "Oooo, hello driver next to me. I'm sucking my pelvic floor muscle and you don't even know it".

Each time you see a red traffic light, add to your 20,000 repetitions practise. You'll notice your 'Endurance Of The Fish' principle strengthens too, and your 'Alignment Of The Serpent' principle becomes stronger, and your lower dantian yin and yang energy begins to feel great. I mean really great, like your whole insides are suddenly alive. And as an addition, your daily red traffic light experience of lifting your pelvic floor muscle and squeezing your bum does wonders for the bedroom activities... say no more!

Energise Your Inner Power

Yin and Yang With Water

Mr Liu is a dazzling man. I know that sounds naff, but he really is. He walks with a satisfied countenance, his movements look breathless as if he was airborne, and he is just down right lovely. He smiles often too, which is great, and even when his face isn't, his eyes are.

I understand why Mr Liu is so content. I can see it when I secretly body scan him; you learnt this skill in 'Endurance Of The Fish'. I'll go through it here to review:

I look at Mr Liu and I can visualise his internal organs. His shoulders are drawn back so he is not compacting his heart into the space between his lungs; his qi is flowing nicely to his large intestine. He is open with a strong latissimus dorsi muscle and he is shining energy from his clavicle (collar bone). His hips and beams are balanced in a triangle with his tailbone, so his liver and gallbladder are functioning efficiently with strong and supportive lumbar muscles. His neck area is long and I can clearly see his inhale and exhale is balanced.

We can visualise the body's organs in relation to the body's posture in the Body Scan exercise. Look at the Wu Xing Interactions diagram, which is found in 'The Wu Xing' chapter. With the knowledge we now have, we can also imagine the body's inner energies and movements. Here we are looking at the kidneys and urinary bladder, your urinary system, which is supported by the water element.

When your body is in balance, your kidneys and urinary bladder (water) are generated by your lungs and large intestine (metal). These are generated by your stomach and spleen (earth). Your stomach and spleen are nourished by your heart and small intestine (fire) which are cared for by your liver and gallbladder (wood). Your liver and gallbladder are both generated by your kidneys and urinary bladder. Your posture is tall and aligned, and your energy harmony goes full circle.

However, you now know that when qi or jing in an element is weak or too strong, the affected element attacks its opposite.

When your kidneys and urinary bladder (water) are lacking nourishment from the metal element, they attack the cardiovascular system: your heart and small intestine (fire). Your fire element is now in disharmony with your kidneys and urinary bladder and so it attacks the respiratory system: your lungs and large intestine (metal). Your metal element then attacks the nervous system: your liver and gallbladder (wood), which then attacks the digestive system: your stomach and spleen (earth).

In TCM, the spleen is regarded as one of the most important organs for healthy digestion – it assists with water metabolism and clears excess fluid from the body. Too much water absorption in the spleen, from attacking the kidneys, creates too much mucus in the metal element; as we saw in 'Co-ordination Of The Horse' with James' frequent colds and rundown energy. The body is now in complete disharmony!

'Control Of The Ox' is associated to the element water. Water is believed to balance the body and it is the element which generates all other elements. When your body is feeling rundown, the water element is the first one you should refer to.

Take a look at the 5 Element Interactions Table in 'The Wu Xing' chapter. You should use this diagram to reference all your findings from the exercises throughout this book. You have performed a Body Scan on yourself in 'Endurance Of The Fish'; you took photographs of yourself for a Postural Assessment in 'Breath Of The Bird'; when looking through the 5 Element Interactions Table, you will notice a lot about your energy when you make reference to your Energy Stress Location Exercise in 'Alignment Of The Serpent'; and your emotions can be connected to the five elements from the Create Your Confidence exercise in 'Co-ordination Of The Horse'.

On The 5 Elements Interaction Table, look at the far right column titled 'Water'. Then look down the column. We can see the effects of weak water element as:

Emotion: Fearful and kind emotions. Have you noticed, as each year passes you have become wearier of doing certain things? You are aware of the consequences, and so you 'tread carefully' with gentleness?

Mental Quality: Erudition, resourcefulness and wit. Do you ever randomly need mental stimulation, such as book learning, joining a new learning course or searching the internet / magazines for quotes of wisdom and intellect?

Sensory Organ: Ears. Are your ears ever unusually sensitive to problems such as tinnitus, a regular build-up of ear wax, ear ache, poor hearing?

Body Part: Bones. Your knees might hurt, you might experience wrist pain, fingers & toes pain, and hip pain.

Body Fluid: Urine. You might also occasionally find yourself with genital and pubic area problems such as STD's, low sex drive, cystitis, water / bladder infections, kidney stones, leaking bladder, and inflammation of your kidneys. You might also notice your body naturally becoming dryer as the years pass. This is because you have occasionally used your reserve pre-natal jing.

Life: Old Age/ Conception. Let's not overlook the results of childbirth. For ladies who have carried a baby, or babies, and have given birth, the water element has experienced quite a shock and has needed a sudden boost of pre-natal jing energy from the kidneys.

If you ignore the signs of weakness within your water element, your body will rapidly show symptoms of forgetfulness, grey hair and lack of elasticity in the skin.

In addition to these symptoms, as your body ages past 35 years, your muscle strength and flexibility will have started to reduce; your major muscle groups will have weakened and relaxed. Especially your abdominal muscles which protect and support your urinary system; the kidneys and urinary bladder AND your lower dantian!

Overly weakened abdominal muscles will create difficulty in curving your upper and middle spine; you will have restriction in proper rotation of your waist; and you will have a bulged frontal abdominal wall, contributing to an over arched lower back. Weakness in your abdominals could create problems with the urinary system and your kidneys / urinary bladder such as difficulty urinating, incomplete urination, urine leakage and possible prolapsed bladder (discomfort or pain in the pelvis).

Oh dear! It is inevitable...

BUT remember: these symptoms are associated to a WEAK water element. If you are aware, which you will be from now on, you will regularly 'check in' with your body, nurture your yin and yang, stimulate your qi energy and dazzle your jing essence so you shimmer with shen!

Mr Liu's 62 year old body is balanced. Everybody can see that because he radiates a glow of shen. Shen is your spirit and shows your overall presence of mind-body connection. When qi and jing are balanced in the body, shen glows!

In TCM, the lower dantian is regarded as the beginning of the energy elixir (qi and jing radiance) process. In Western physiology, the lower abdominal area is the location of the pelvic floor muscle. They are both the same thing!

'Control Of The Ox' focuses on engaging your pelvic floor muscle / lower dantian and strengthens your abdominal muscles to support and protect your urinary system, opening the meridians to your kidneys and urinary bladder – the foundation of your qi and jing balance and shimmering shen!

Execute Lifting And Squeezing

'Pillow Pilates' Pelvic Floor Morning Movement

By strengthening your abdominal muscles, your back and pelvic floor muscle; you are supporting and protecting your kidney and urinary bladder. 'The Hundreds' is the absolute perfect movement to do for lower dantian strength, stimulation and mind-body connection.

Here I've written the instructions to 'The Hundreds' in clear and concise stages for you to follow. Simple reminder instructions, for you to copy if you feel following these instructions are too detailed, are at the back of this book in the 'What Next?' chapter. These instructions are here for you to fully understand the movements and breath work involved.

Before you begin, make sure to engage the five principles you now know: *pull tall through the crown of your head, draw your shoulders back, tilt your pelvis in-line, suck your belly button into your spine* and *lift your pelvic floor muscle & squeeze your bum.*

Lay on your back on top of your mattress with your arms resting at your sides; and bend your knees so your feet are flat on the mattress. Make sure your feet are hip distance apart - you need your pelvis to be aligned and you should feel long through your tailbone.

Breathe in through your nose to fill your lungs. As you breathe out lengthen through your fingers to reach towards your toes, your arms should be lifted off the mattress in-line with your hips.

On the exhale, tuck your chin into your chest, with a nice big double chin, and roll your head off the mattress so you are looking through your thighs. Open your occipital in the base of your skull and keep your shoulders down away from your ears. Your chin must be over your chest. Make sure you are totally relaxed in your neck muscles.

Breathe in to stretch your tailbone and fingers, with length through your elbows, towards your feet. Suck your belly button into your spine and work your pelvic floor muscle. You will feel really strong around your waist when you have this position correct. A great visualisation I use for this feeling to click into action is to imagine you have a 1980's thick elastic belt around your waist from your ribs to your hips. Keep the elastic belt comfortable, don't let it stretch wide. Your ribs and hips should be in-line.

Breathe in through your nose for five counts. These are short breaths where you fill your lungs gradually so that on the fifth inhale your lungs and external intercostal muscles are fully expanded wide – remember from 'Co-ordination Of The Horse' to make sure you're breathing laterally and not lifting your front.

Breathe out to engage your internal intercostal muscles with five short controlled out breaths. By the third short exhale you should feel your pelvic floor muscle lifting and your abdominal muscles tightening and pulling towards your spine.

On each short inhale and exhale breath you should bounce your arms just enough to feel your latissimus dorsi muscle engage. I call this action a pulse because it is a rhythm keeping your breaths and upper body controlled.

Repeat for 10 full sets of five inhales and five exhales. So in total you are breathing and pulsing your arms 100 times.

To finish, inhale a deep long breath to hold the roll up position. Keeping your abdominals sucked in to your spine and your chin tucked into your chest, with a beautiful double chin, lengthen your tailbone and arms towards your feet. Exhale to slowly roll your head back down to the mattress. DO NOT let your shoulders creep up to your ears. Do keep the open length through your neck. Relax your arms and gently drop your legs down to the mattress.

Take a deep breath in to fill every inch of your body, even the heels of your feet! Take a few moments to bring your breathing back to normal before you start your usual morning activity.

ATTENTION: Visualise sliding your ribs towards your hips on your roll up while keeping long through your tailbone – don't let your lower back curve. This ensures your abdominals are flat, your energy is strong in your pelvic floor muscle, and you are engaging your pelvis tilt in-line with your hips.

WARNING: You might experience neck ache during the Hundreds exercise. If you feel you are straining your neck muscles, gently lower your head, on an exhale, to the mattress. Make sure to continue the pulsing of your arms and lengthen long through the back of your neck. Keep practising the head roll, it is a case of practise makes perfect. As you roll your head, tuck your chin into your chest so you have a beautiful double chin. It is the chin jutting out to start your movement which gives you a neck strain feeling.

'Control Of The Ox' works your pelvic floor muscle; strengthening your abdominals and your lower dantian which opens the meridians to your qi in your kidneys and bladder, boosting your body's urinary system detox process and the release of post-natal jing around your body, creating dazzling vibrant health and a glowing shen shine, just like Mr Liu!

'The Wu Xing'

Traditional Chinese Medicine

The Wu Xing Interactions

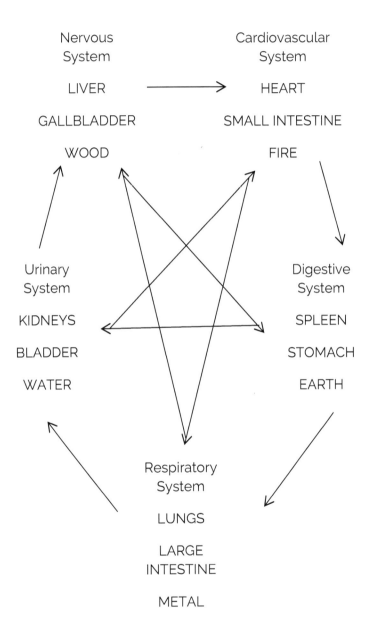

Nervous System
LIVER
GALLBLADDER
WOOD

Cardiovascular System
HEART
SMALL INTESTINE
FIRE

Urinary System
KIDNEYS
BLADDER
WATER

Digestive System
SPLEEN
STOMACH
EARTH

Respiratory System
LUNGS
LARGE INTESTINE
METAL

The 5 Element Interactions

	Endurance Of The Fish	Breath Of The Bird	Alignment Of The Serpent	Co-ordination Of The Horse	Control Of The Ox
Element	Wood	Fire	Earth	Metal	Water
Mental Quality	Impulsive & Curious	Passion & Intensity	Willingness & Honesty	Intuition & Rationality	Erudition & Wit
Emotion	Anger & Kindness	Hate & Resolve	Anxiety & Joy	Grief & Bravery	Fear & Kindness
Yin Organ	Liver	Heart	Spleen	Lungs	Kidneys
Yang Organ	Gallbladder	Small Intestine	Stomach	Large Intestine	Urinary Bladder
Sensory Organ	Eyes	Tongue	Mouth	Nose	Ears
Body Part	Tendons	Pulse	Muscles	Skin	Bones
Body Fluid	Tears	Sweat	Saliva	Mucus	Urine
Finger	Index Finger	Middle Finger	Thumb	Ring Finger	Little Finger
Sense	Sight	Taste	Touch	Smell	Hearing
Taste	Sour	Bitter	Sweet	Pungent	Salty
Colour	Green	Red	Yellow	White	Black
Life	Early Childhood	Pre-Puberty	Adolescence	Adulthood	Old Age
Body System	Nervous	Cardio-vascular	Digestive	Respiratory	Urinary
Season	Spring	Summer	Solstice	Autumn	Winter

The Yellow Emperor said

"The ruler as well as the masses share their upmost desire:

the wish for a perfect body."

- The Yellow Emperor's
Classic of Internal Medicine

What Now?

Practise Makes Perfect

The 10,000 Repetition Theory

Pillow Pilates Morning Movement Routine

Each morning before getting out of bed, energise your body with this quick 10-minute routine:

Arm Circles: Sit tall on top of your mattress. Cross your arms over your hips (left hand on right hip, right hand on left hip). Breathe in to slowly bring your arms up over your head, as though taking a jumper off. Breathe out to stretch your arms out to the sides as you lower your arms back to the starting position. Repeat 10 times.

Spine Twist: Sit tall on top of your mattress. Your legs are stretched in front of you and your arms are mirroring your legs, palms face down. Breathe in to pulse your right elbow to twist your ribs to your right side. Breathe in again to twist from your spine, looking over your right shoulder. Exhale to return to the start position. Repeat the twist and look over your left shoulder. Return to the start position on your exhale. Repeat 5 times each side.

Single Leg Stretch: Slowly lower your body down to lay on your back on top of your mattress, with your knees bent and your arms by your sides. Breathe out to lift your right leg in a 90 degree bend over your right hip, with your five principles engaged. Exhale to stretch your right leg away from your centre, keeping your foot in-line with your hip. Breathe in to bend your right knee over your hip. Exhale to stretch your right leg away from your centre, keeping your foot in-line with your hip. Repeat 10 times. Exhale to lower your right foot down to the mattress, with a bent knee, before repeating the routine with your left leg.

Hundreds: Stay laying on your back. Breathe in to stretch your arms at your sides. Breathe out to roll your head up and over your chest to look through your thighs. Keep your eyes looking through your legs. Breathe in for five counts and breathe out for five counts, bouncing your arms on every breath. Suck your belly button into your spine, engage your pelvic floor muscle. Repeat 10 times, so you are completing 100 arm bounces in total. Breathe in to hold your position in stillness before exhaling to lower your head back down to the mattress.

Lateral Leg Lift Routine:

Lateral Leg Lift Abduction: Roll over to lay on your right side, with your right hand stretching above your head, in-line with your ears. Keep your waist engaged to feel your diamond waist under your lowest rib. Breathe in to lift your left leg to hip level. Breathe out to lower with control. Repeat 10 times.

Lateral Leg Lift Adduction: Stay on your right side. Breathe in to lift your left leg to hip level, breathe in again to lift your right leg to meet your left leg. Keep both legs squeezing together and slowly lower both legs to the mattress with control on your exhale. Repeat 10 times. Roll over onto your left side to repeat the Lateral Leg Lift Routine with your right leg.

To finish, hug your knees into your chest. Take some deep breaths to relax before stretching your whole body, ready to start your day with energy and a clear mind :-)

Body-Mind Exercises

These exercises help you connect to your body again. They help you remember why you need a powerful posture to gain vibrant health.

Body Scan; Endurance Of The Fish.

Practise this exercise as often as possible, but be subtle in your people watching! When you get chance, take a moment to casually observe someone and imagine the positioning of their vital organs. As you look at them, visualize their internal mechanics, see in your mind the connections of their body systems and their body muscles working with their posture.

Postural Assessment; Breath Of The Bird.

Do this exercise once every three months, or so. If you wish to do it more often, that's ok :-) By looking at yourself in standing, you can determine how you feel, what injuries you have or had in the past and areas of the body which may cause problems in the future.

Energy Stress Location Exercise; Alignment Of The Serpent.

This exercise is a good one to practise once a week to ground your thoughts and connect to your inner self again. What mood do you feel before you engage your powerful posture? What difference can you feel once all five powerful posture principles are engaged?

Create Your Own Confidence; Co-ordination Of The Horse.

I love this exercise, so I would say do it every day if you can. But I appreciate not everyone is as extrovert as I can be (cringe). Do practise this one, but do it when you feel comfortable to – maybe once a month. Take on the characteristics of a super strong person - someone who impresses you, and adopt the posture that person holds.

Ride The Wave; Control Of The Ox.

Definitely do this one every day! Train your body-mind connection by focusing on your pelvic floor muscle.

Nutrition

Of course what you eat plays a huge role in your body's energy, health and vitality. Follow this simple guide for improving your health and overall wellbeing. Note: This list is not endless, it is purely an introduction to better choice foods that are simple to add to your daily meals.

	Endurance Of The Fish	Breath Of The Bird	Alignment Of The Serpent	Co-ordination Of The Horse	Control Of The Ox
Element and Organs	Wood Liver & Gallbladder	Fire Heart & Small Intestine	Earth Spleen & Stomach	Metal Lungs & Large Intestine	Water Kidneys & Bladder
Taste	Sour Foods	Bitter Foods	Sweet Foods	Pungent Foods	Salty Foods
Colour	Green Foods such as:	Red Foods such as:	Yellow Foods such as:	White Foods such as:	Black Foods such as:
	Mung Bean	Carrots	Sweet Corn	Onion	Eggplant
	Leeks	Tomatoes	Pumpkin	Tofu	Seaweed
	Broccoli	Sweet Potatoes	Butternut Squash	Bamboo Shoots	Purple Cabbage
	Green Apples & Grapes	Strawberries & Red Apples	Pineapple & Starfruit	Banana	Raisins & Black Grapes
	Coriander	Chilies	Lemon	Garlic	Shiitake Mush-rooms
	Green lentils	Red Beans (Adzuki Beans)	Peanuts	Rice & Noodles	Black Peas & Black Beans
	Green Pepper	Red Pepper	Yellow Pepper	White Radish	Figs & Dates

Finish

Embrace Your Connections

We're at the end of our 'The Way You Move Says It All' talk together. I'm so thrilled that you have been interested to let me share this information with you.

I know there is an awful lot of content here, and I do not expect you to remember it all. If you could take away just one thing, though, I hope it would be to engage all five 'Feel Alive System' principles:

Pull tall through the crown of your head

Draw your shoulders back

Suck your tummy in

Tilt your pelvis in-line

Squeeze your bum and pelvic floor muscle.

Now, go on out into the beautiful world with strong, agile, free and easy movement; and just as ancient folk in China did thousands of years ago, take time to notice that everything is connected to everything else. You are worthy of connecting to your protecting dragon and your inner power. Embrace your powerful posture every day!

About The Author

Jessica Blackbond

Born and raised in Yorkshire, UK; Jessica graduated from university in Leeds and danced professionally both onstage and for the television. In her late 20's, while travelling the globe, she became inspired to open a dance and fitness studio centred on the ethos of 'exciting and enthusing people from all walks of life to be committed to looking good and feeling great'.

Trained in the Graham Technique, Classical Pilates, Holistic Massage Therapy and Traditional Chinese Medicine Reflexology, Jessica has honed her skills to focus on her passion of body posture and the benefits of holding oneself correctly with powerful posture.

Jessica wrote this book during a two year sabbatical in China, where she learnt the principles and methodology of Traditional Chinese Medicine Reflexology. It was in China where she discovered the Tao philosophy of the five elements of nature and the interdependence of yin and yang. And it was in China where inspiration struck to combine her TCM and Pilates knowledge to create a website specifically for men and women to help reduce body stress, prevent disease, and manage emotional moods in an alternative format.

Jessica teaches more Traditional Chinese Medicine knowledge, self-help exercises and 24 Classic Pilates 'Pillow Pilates Morning Movements' in her 6-week online 'Feel Alive System' Program. For more information, please visit People Move Stress Less website: www. peoplemovestressless .com

If I was your personal fitness trainer at home, when would you want me to train you… in the morning or evening? Join my 9-hour video course and get access to my teaching at any time day or night!

Learn all about Pilates, posture, and how to care for your body so it works like a well-oiled machine - for life.

Plus, you'll get lifetime access to content, you can learn on any device at your own pace, and you're protected by my 100% money back guarantee.

Sign up at

WWW.PEOPLEMOVESTRESSLESS.COM

'THE FEEL ALIVE SYSTEM

6-WEEK ONLINE PROGRAM'

LEARN CHINESE MEDICINE PRACTISES:

EYE EXERCISES

- Quickly relieve tired eyes and headache

MERIDIAN TAPPING

- Bring blood flow to the skin and remove toxins

DETOXING FOOD SNACKS

- Food grouping helps in the processing of jing & qi

THREE DIMENSIONAL BREATHING

- Improve sleep and relax the mind

FOOT SOAK AND MASSAGE

- Boost your body's natural ability to heal itself

www.peoplemovestressless.com/courses/pilates-and-chinese-medicine-combined-for-a-younger-feeling-healthier-you

Printed in Great Britain
by Amazon